Encyclopedia
of Design

Encyclopedia
of Design

HART

HART PUBLISHING COMPANY
NEW YORK CITY

LIBRARY OF CONGRESS CATALOG CARD NO. 82-83615
ISBN 0-8055-1276-4 (Paperback 0-8055-0452-4)
MANUFACTURED IN THE UNITED STATES OF AMERICA

CONTENTS

HOW TO USE THIS BOOK

ENCYCLOPEDIA OF DESIGN is a collection of hundreds of pictures of many periods and cultures.

All these pictures are in the public domain, and may be used for any purpose without fee or permission. Most of the pictures derive from books and magazines for which copyright is not in force.

So as not to clutter a caption, the source is given an abbreviated designation. Full publication data may be found in the *Sources* section, in which all sources are listed in alphabetical order, with the full title of the book or magazine, the publisher, and the date of publication. The *Sources* section commences on page 430.

Encyclopedia
of Design

African Designs

Wooden mask, Congo-Kinshasa. *African Designs.*

Ashanti printing stamp, Ghana. *African Designs.*

African Designs.

Zulu carved wooden figure, Republic of South Africa. *African Designs.*

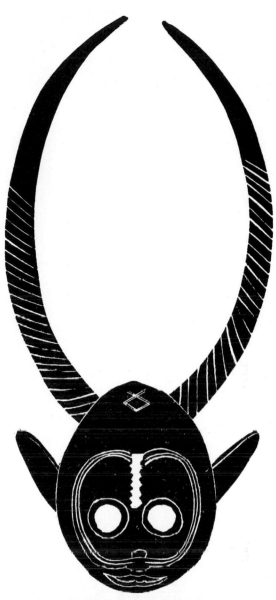

Wooden mask from Mali. *African Designs.*

Sundi woven mat design from the lower Congo area. *African Designs.*

American Designs

Early 19th century quilt from Pennsylvania. *Source unknown*

19th century floral design. *Early American*

American Designs continued

Various embroidery motifs from an 18th century Massachusetts quilt. *Early American*

Various embroidery motifs from an 18th century Massachusetts quilt. *Early American*

American Designs continued

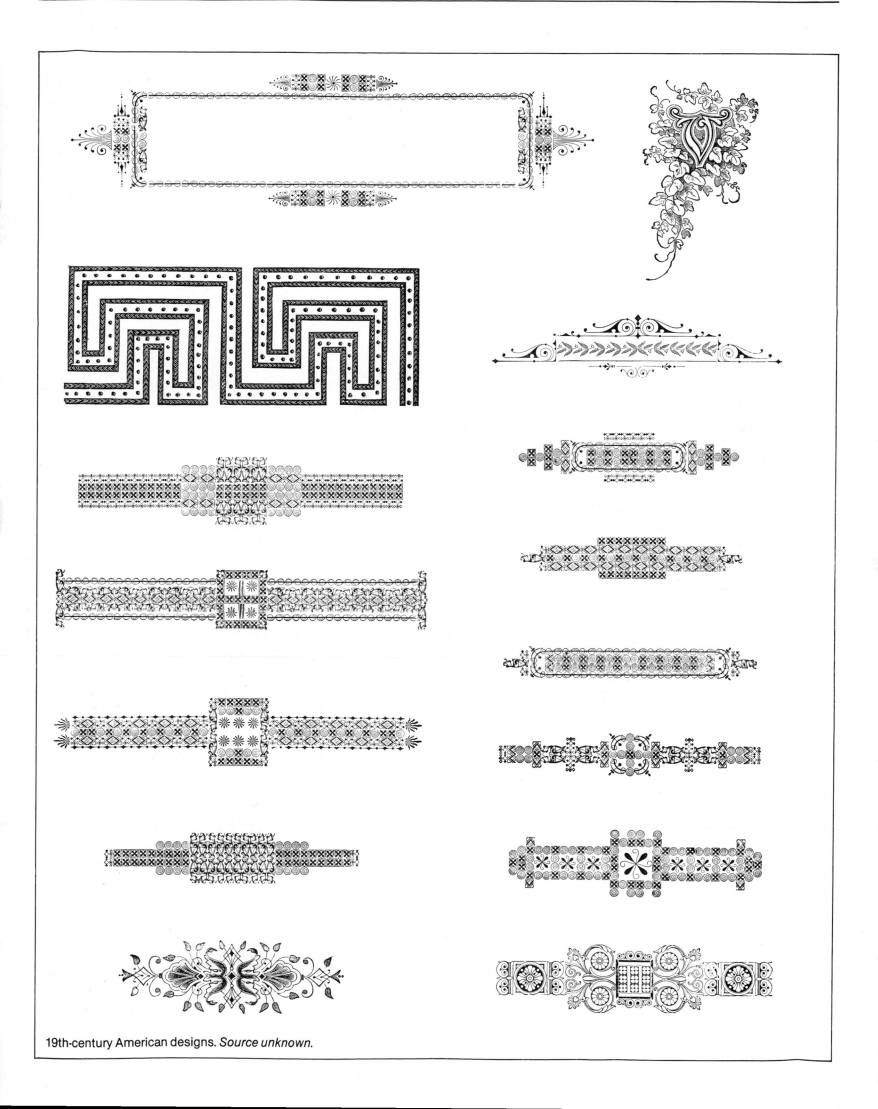

19th-century American designs. *Source unknown.*

American Designs continued

Sofa cushion decorated with Sorrento embroidery. *Needle and Brush.*

Monogram. *Needle and Brush.*

Needle and Brush.

Decorated chair. *Needle and Brush.*

Pitcher in Royal Worcester style. *Needle and Brush.*

Table, with cover. *Needle and Brush.*

Embroidered table cover. *Needle and Brush.*

Blotter holder. *Needle and Brush.*

American Designs continued

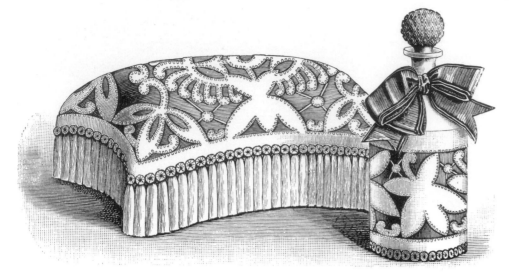

Cushion and bottle. *Needle and Brush.*

Chair with embroidered cushions. *Needle and Brush.*

Fancy pen wiper. *Needle and Brush.*

Applique. *Needle and Brush.*

Shelf drapery. *Needle and Brush.*

Allover Patterns

American Indian Designs

Chilkat blanket: bear and killer-whales. *Design and Decoration*

Haida designs. *Source unknown*

Headdress of the Tsimshian tribe.
Design and Decoration

Haida design. *Source unknown*

Haida totem pole.
Design and Decoration

House of the Haida tribe. *Design and Decoration*

American Indian Designs continued

Modern Hopi potter design. *Decorative Art*

Pottery design from Sia, New Mexico. *Decorative Art*

Pueblo pottery design. *Decorative Art*

Design from piece of pottery found
in Utah. *Authentic Indian Designs*

Pueblo pottery design from Tusayan.
Authentic Indian Designs

Pueblo pottery design, based on corn blades. *Decorative Art*

Pueblo pottery design. *Decorative Art*

Pueblo pottery
design.
Decorative Art

Water vase of the Zuni tribe. *Authentic Indian Designs*

Modern Hopi pottery design. *Decorative Art*

Conventionalized border pattern for Pueblo pottery. *Decorative Art*

American Indian Designs continued

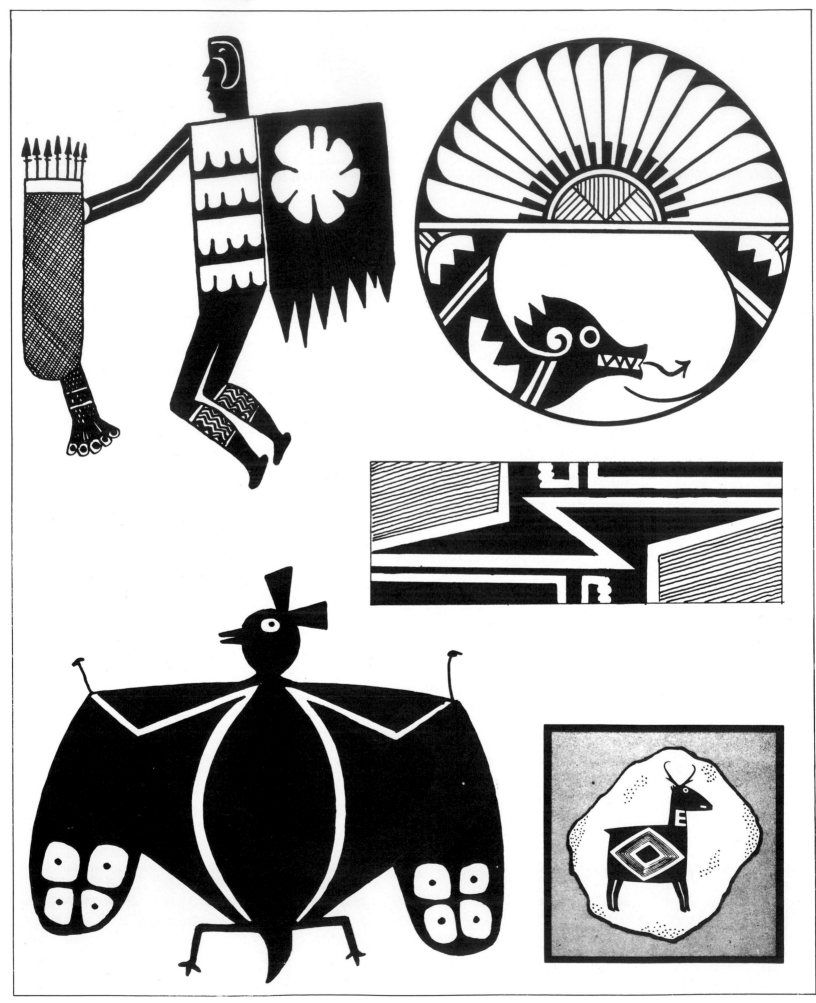

Mimbres design. *Mimbres Design Calendar.*

Mimbres design. *Mimbres Design Calendar.*

American Indian Designs continued

Zuni pottery. *Ethnology*

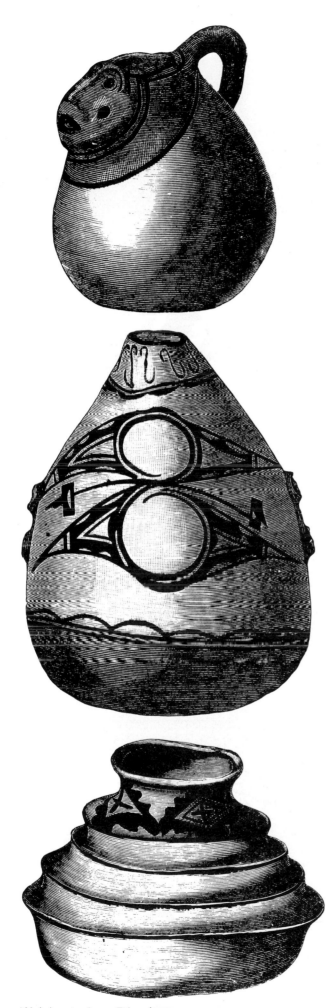

Wolpi statuette and vase. *Ethnology*

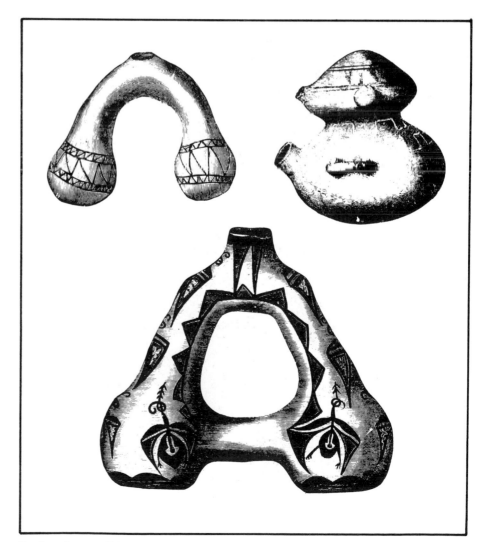

Wolpi water jars. *Ethnology*

Zuni canteens. *Ethnology*

American Indian Designs continued

Zuni woman polishing pottery. *Ethnology*

Chiriquian alligator ware. *Ethnology*

Laguna water vessels. *Ethnology*

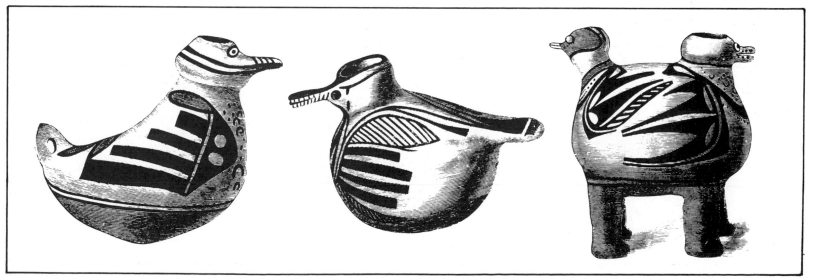

Laguna animal effigies. *Ethnology*

American Indian Designs continued

Mimbres Designs. *Museum of San Lorenzo, New Mexico.*

Mimbres Designs. *Museum of San Lorenzo, New Mexico.*

Art Nouveau Designs

Art Nouveau, Menten.   *Art Nouveau, Menten.*   *Art Nouveau, Menten.*

Art Nouveau, Menten.　　　*Art Nouveau, Menten.*　　　*Art Nouveau, Menten.*

Art Nouveau Designs continued

Art Nouveau book ornament. *Studio*

Art Nouveau book ornament. *Studio*

Assyrian Designs

Border designs, two examples. *Hart Publishing*

Bas-relief. *L'Art, Vol. 24*

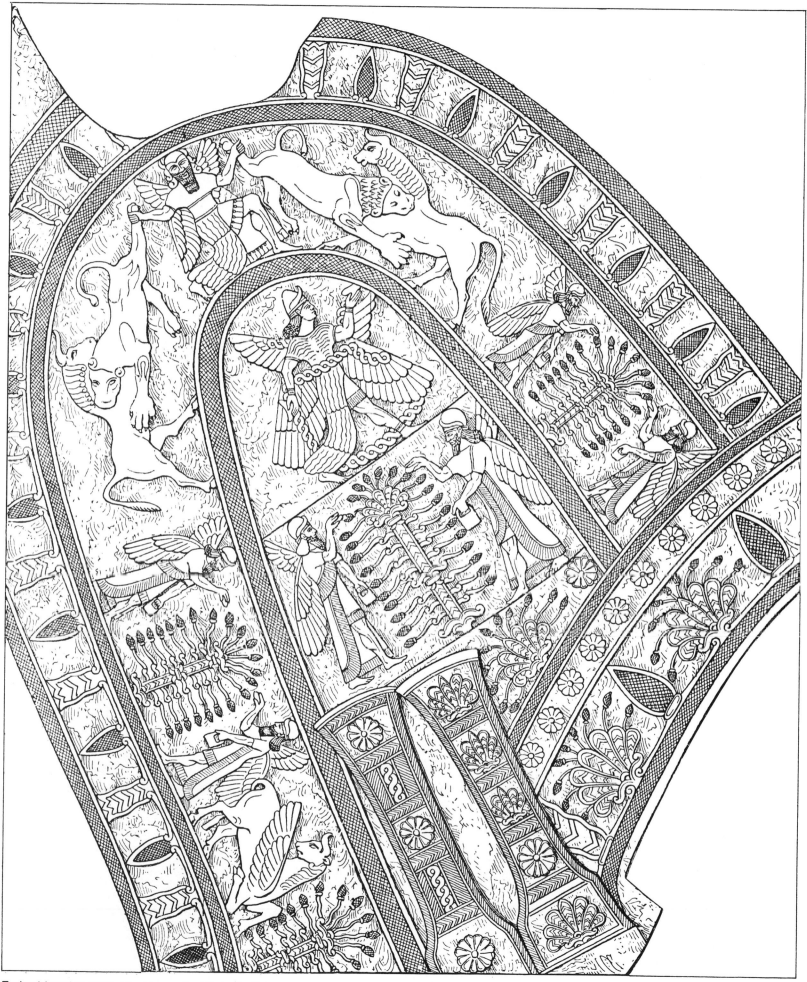

Embroidered mantle of a monarch. *Historic Ornament*

Assyrian Designs continued

Statue of a winged deity found at Nimrod, dating from 800 B.C. *London News, Vol. 17*

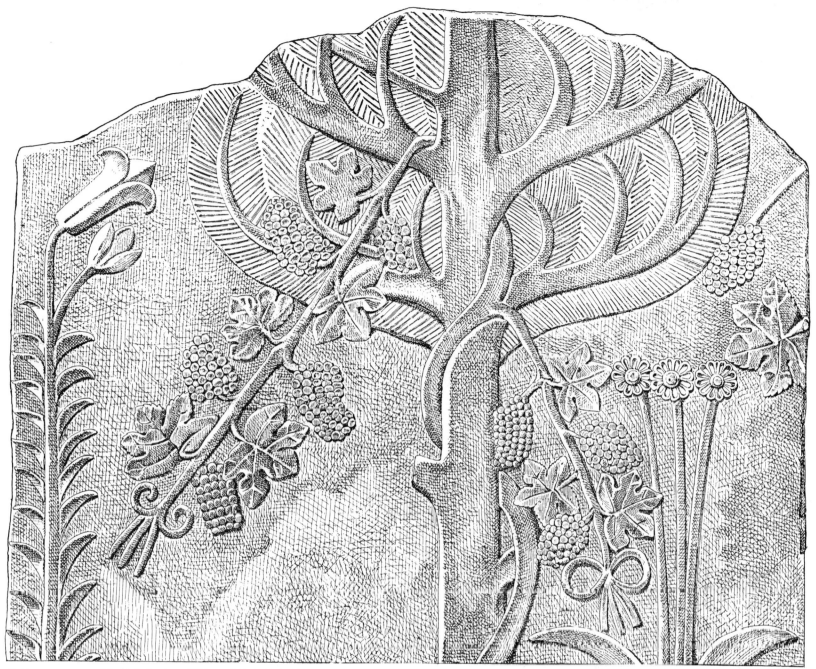

Foliage on a marble relief, circa 650 B.C. *L'Art, Vol. 13*

Assyrian court officials, from a relief. *Sunday Book*

Assyrian Designs continued

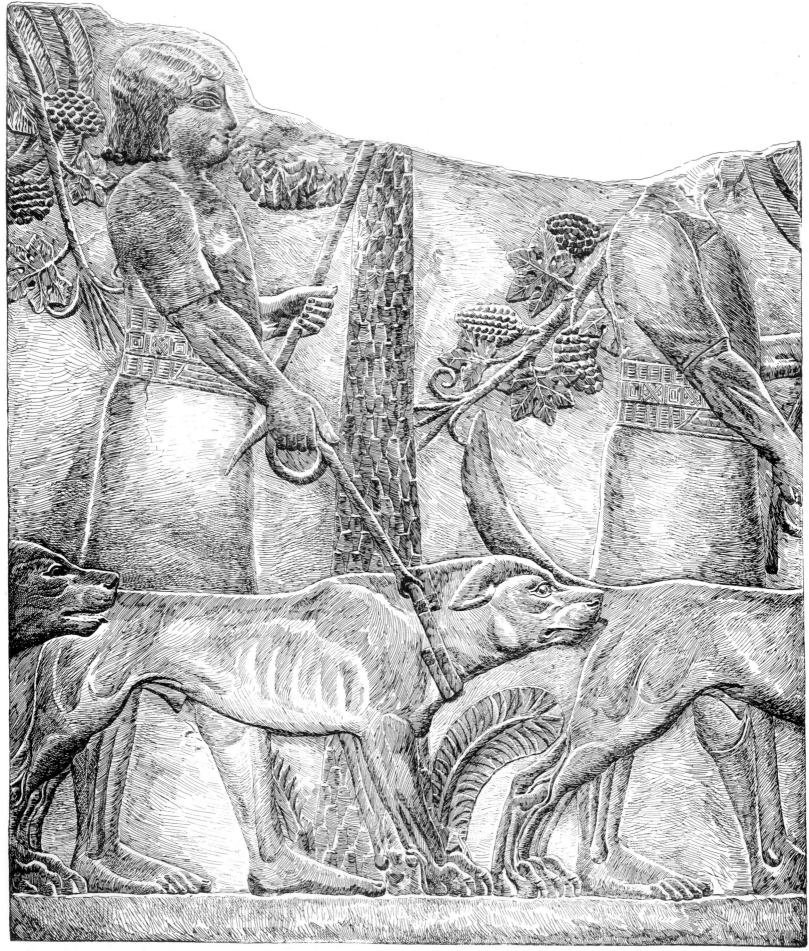

Hunting scene, bas-relief fragment. *L'Art, Vol. 21*

Bronze platter. *Historic Ornament*

Attire of a king. *La vie privee*

Winged bull from Nineveh. *Voyages & Travels, Vol. 1*

British Designs

Inlaid ornament. *Gewerbehalle, Vol. 6*

Table cloth design by C. Berger, late 19th century. *Gewerbehalle, Vol. 2*

Porcelain design. *Gewerbehalle, Vol. 7*

Carved wood ornament, 15th century. *Encyclopedia of Ornament*

British Designs continued

Ante-pendiums, early 16th century. *Encyclopedia of Ornament*

Border of lace veil. *Industry of Nations*

Embroidered waistcoat.
Industry of Nations

Irish damask napkin. *Industry of Nations*

Victorian Stencils

British Designs continued

Material for a cashmere dress, made in Scotland. *Industry of Nations*

Ribbon. *Industry of Nations*

Victorian Stencils

Celtic interlaced ornament. *Outlines*

Gold brocade pattern. *Industry of Nations*

British Designs continued

Four stained glass window designs based on oak and maple leaf motifs, Canterbury Cathedral. *Encyclopedia of Ornament*

Scottish cradle cover. *Industry of Nations*

British Designs continued

Silk pattern. *Industry of Nations*

Furniture damask. *Industry of Nations*

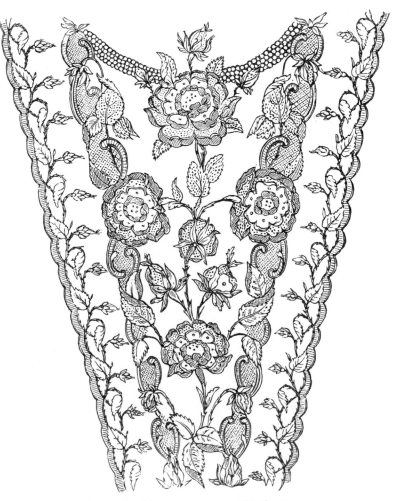

Scottish chemise embroidery. *Industry of Nations*

Poplin pattern. *Industry of Nations*

Ribbon. *Industry of Nations*

Carpet design. *Industry of Nations*

Motif for wool design. *Industry of Nations*

Victorian Stencils

British Designs continued

Ancient porcelain plate. *L'Art, Vol. 33*

Vignettes from velvet hangings, late 6th century.
Encyclopedia of Ornament.

Sixteenth century lace pattern. *Encyclopedia of Ornament*

Cashmere scarf, made in Scotland. *Industry of Nations*

British Designs continued

Irish drapery design. *Gewerbehalle, Vol. 12*

Painted ornament for a railway carriage. *Workshop, Vol. 2*

British Designs continued

Crystal Palace.

Crystal Palace.

Crystal Palace.

Crystal Palace.

Crystal Palace.

British Designs continued

Medieval diaper ornament, four examples. *Outlines*

Embroidered cloth. *Industry of Nations*

Table cloth, one corner. *Industry of Nations*

British Designs continued

Carpet design by F.T. Parris. *Industry of Nations*

Brocaded silk by Lewis & Allenby, of London. *Industry of Nations*

Embroidery trimming. *Industry of Nations*

Stained glass window, York Cathedral. *Encyclopedia of Ornament*

British Designs continued

Archbishop's cape. *Industry of Nations*

Three stencil designs. *Victorian Stencils*

British Designs continued

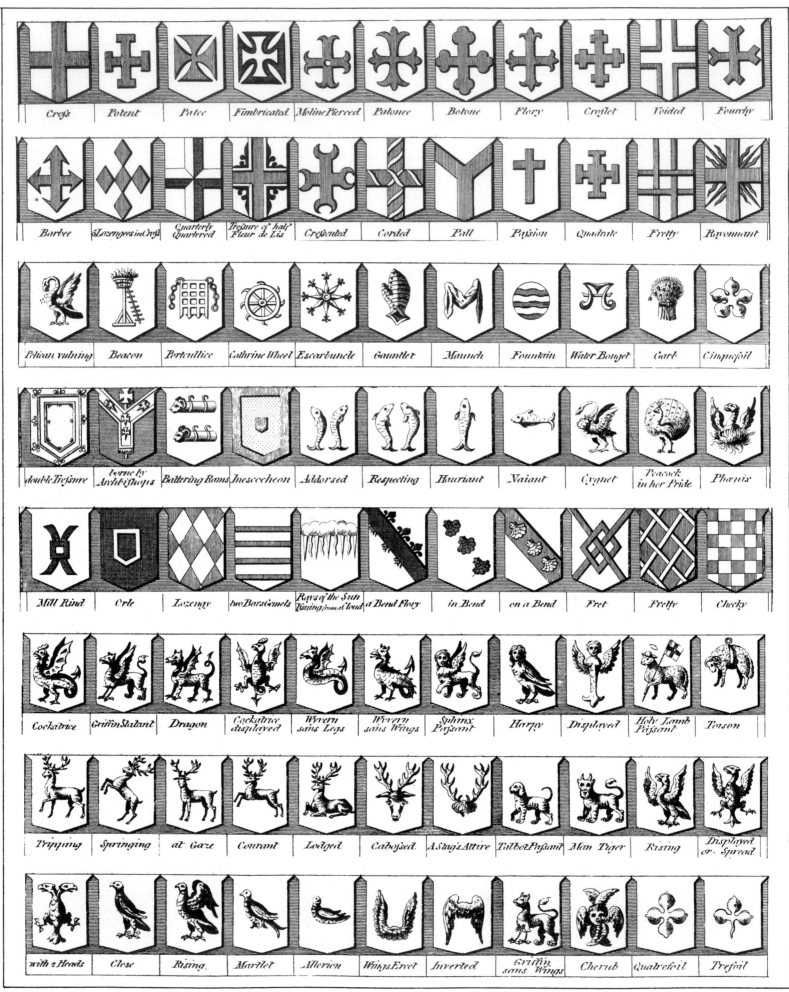

Cross	Potent	Patee	Fimbricated	Moline Pierced	Patonce	Botone	Flory	Croslet	Voided	Fourchy
Barbee	5 Lozenges in Cross	Quarterly Quartered	Tressure of half Fleur de Lis	Cressented	Corded	Pall	Passion	Quadrate	Fretty	Rayonnant
Pelican vulning	Beacon	Portcullice	Cathrine Wheel	Escarbuncle	Gauntlet	Maunch	Fountain	Water Bouget	Garb	Cinquefoil
double Tressure	borne by Archbishops	Battering Rams	Inescocheon	Addorsed	Respecting	Hauriant	Naiant	Cygnet	Peacock in her Pride	Phœnix
Mill Rind	Orle	Lozengy	two Barstemels	Rays of the Sun rising from a Cloud	a Bend Flory	in Bend	on a Bend	Fret	Fretty	Checky
Cockatrice	Griffin Statant	Dragon	Cockatrice displayed	Wivern sans Legs	Wivern sans Wings	Sphinx Prissant	Harpy	Displayed	Holy Lamb Prissant	Toison
Tripping	Springing	at Gaze	Courant	Lodged	Caboysed	A Stag's Attire	Talbot Prissant	Man Tiger	Rising	Displayed or Spread
with 2 Heads	Close	Rising	Martlet	Allerion	Wings Erect	Inverted	Griffin sans Wings	Cherub	Quatrefoil	Trefoil

Heraldic charges. *English Encyclopedia*

Painted ornament for a railway carriage. *Gewerbehalle, Vol. 6*

Carved ornament on a box, late 15th century. *Encyclopedia of Ornament*

British Designs continued

Design for Schools.

Design for Schools.

Design for Schools.

Design for Schools.

British Designs continued

Design for Schools.

Design for Schools.

Design for Schools.

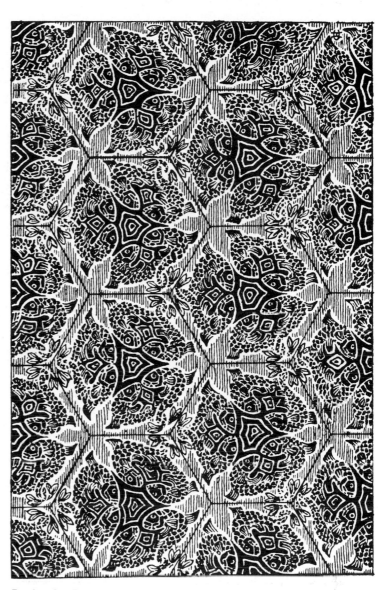

Design for Schools.

Design for Schools.

British Designs continued

Design for Schools.

Design for Schools.

Design for Schools.

Design for Schools.

Design for Schools.

Design for Schools.

British Designs continued

Design for Schools.

Design for Schools.

Design for Schools.

Design for Schools.

Design for Schools.

Design for Schools.

Design for Schools.

British Designs continued

Woodcut by Gertrude Hermes. *Studio*

Ribbon. *Industry of Nations*

Silk design. *Industry of Nations*

Heraldic lion, 13th century. *Pattern Design*

British Designs continued

Encyclopedia of Ornament.

Design for Schools.

Design for Schools.

An iron grill based on the holly. *Design for Schools.*

British Designs continued

Design for Schools.

Design for Schools.

Design for Schools.

Design for Schools.

British Designs continued

Design for Schools.

Design for Schools.

Design for Schools.

Design for Schools.

Worcester porcelain, 1751. *Symbols, Signs & Signets.*

Design for Schools.

Design for Schools.

Design for Schools.

Design for Schools.

British Designs continued

Encyclopedia of Ornament.

Early Grisaille glass, Salisbury Cathedral. *Glazier.*

Encyclopedia of Ornament.

Border from the Grenville Sporziada,
circa 1490. *British Museum.*

Design for Schools.

Celtic Designs continued

Book of Kells. *University of Dublin.*

Book of Durrow. *University of Dublin.*

Book of Kells. *University of Dublin.*

Book of Kells.
University of Dublin.

Chinese Designs

Plum blossom and magpie, embroidery design. *Folk Designs*

Carp leaping the Dragon Gate to become dragons, embroidery design. *Folk Designs*

Papercut Design

Carpet design with pheonix, 16th century. *L'Art, Vol. 24*

Chinese Designs continued

Parrot. *Chinese Folk Designs.*

Woven silk, 18th century. *Glazier.*

Symbol signs. *Symbols, Signs & Signets.*

Woven silk, 18th century. *Glazier.*

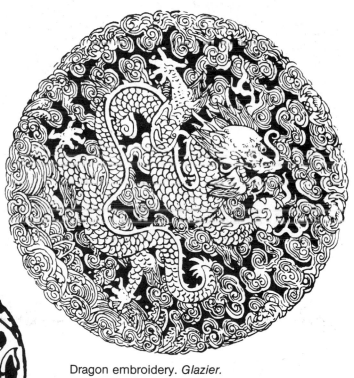

Dragon embroidery. *Glazier.*

Glazier.

Chinese Designs continued

Squirrel and grapes. *Papercut Design*

Papercut Design

Ancient tapestry. *L'Art, Vol. 37* □

Papercut Design

Ancient tapestry. *L'Art, Vol. 37* □

Rabbit *Papercut Design*

Papercut Design

Papercut Design

Chinese Designs continued

Woodcut. *Bamboo Studio*

Tsao **Pondweed**	**Hu** **Tiger**	**Shan** **Mountains**	**Hsi** **Double Joy**
T'u **Hare**	**Shu** **Rat**	**Shih** **Boar**	**Hou** **Monkey**
Sung **Pine Tree**	**Chu** **Bamboo**	**Shih** **Persimmon**	**Li** **Pear**
Niu **Ox**	**Hsiang** **Elephant**	**Yang Yin** **Dual Principle**	**Shou** **Longevity**

Various folk motifs. *Folk Designs*

Chinese Designs continued

French plate, 18th century. *L'Art, Vol. 23*

Papercut Design

Papercut Design

Chinese Designs continued

Diaper Ornament. *Outlines*

Diaper Ornament. *Outlines*

Chinese Designs continued

Hart Publishing

Moonlit landscape. *Folk Designs*

Dschang Guo, the patron saint of doctors. seated on a white ass. *Chinesische Teppich*

Ho Sian-Gu, the patron saint of housewives, with a lotus flower. *Chinesische Teppich*

Chrysanthemum. *Papercut Design*

Chinese Designs continued

Fabric design. *Chinesische Teppich*

臨流
十竹齋寫

Woodcut.*Bamboo Studio*

Coptic Designs

Embroidered ornament. *L'Art* & *Coptic Textiles*

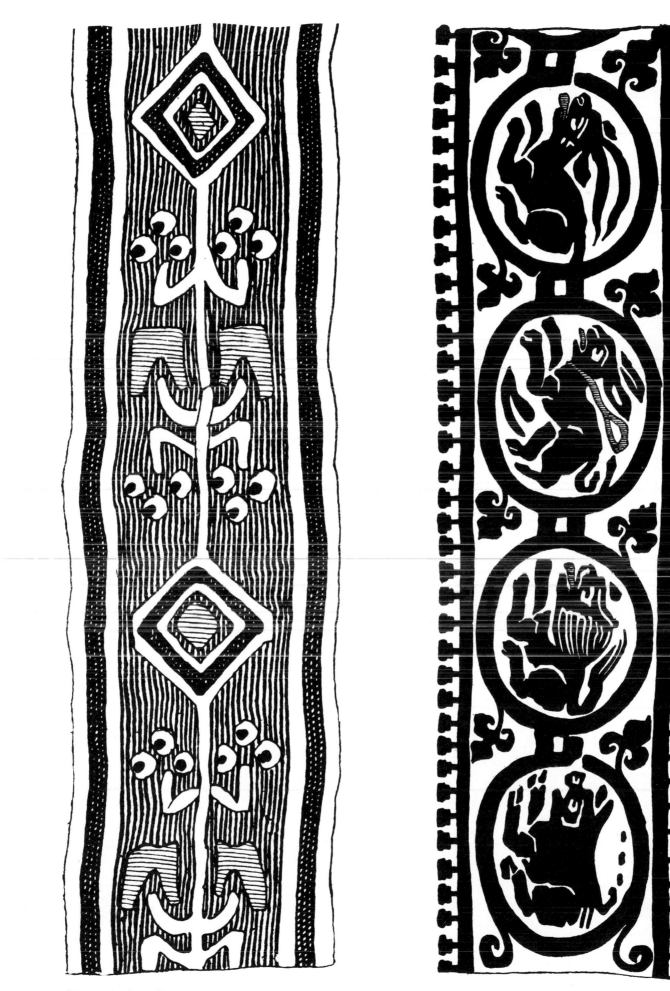

Border design. *Coptic Textiles*

Border design. *Coptic Textiles*

Egyptian Designs continued

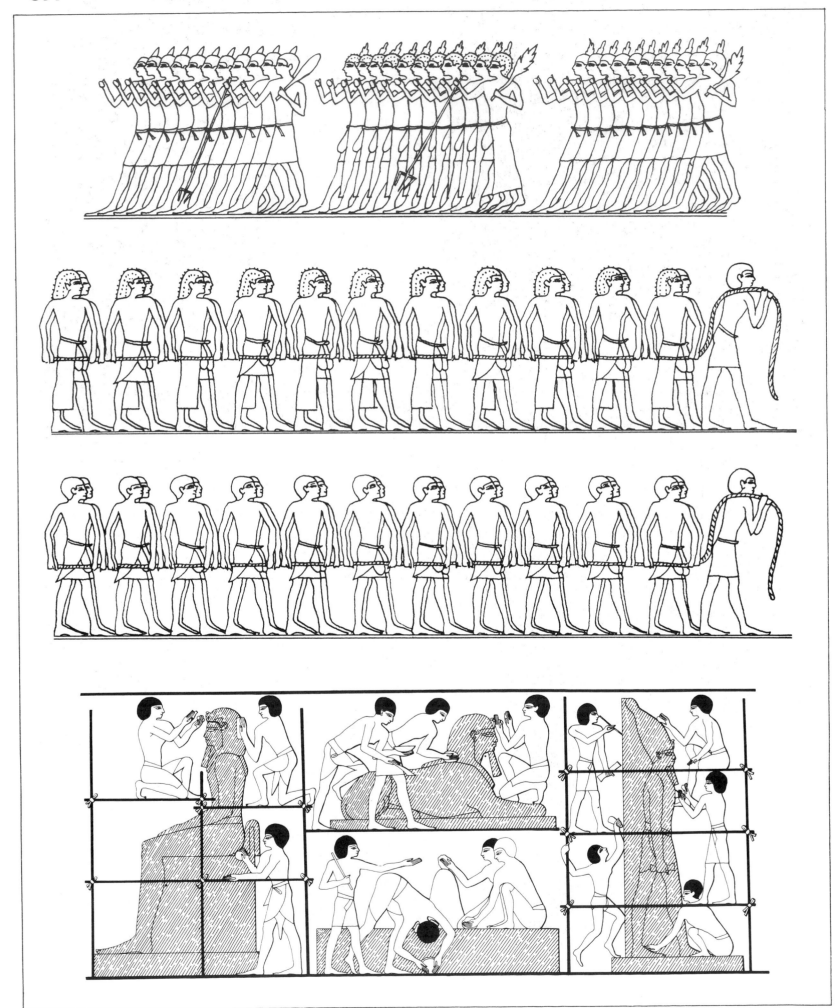

Workers sculpting and transporting monuments, depicted on tomb walls. *Century, Various Vols.*

Incarnations of Isis. *Source Illustrations*

Osiris enthroned. *Industrial Arts*

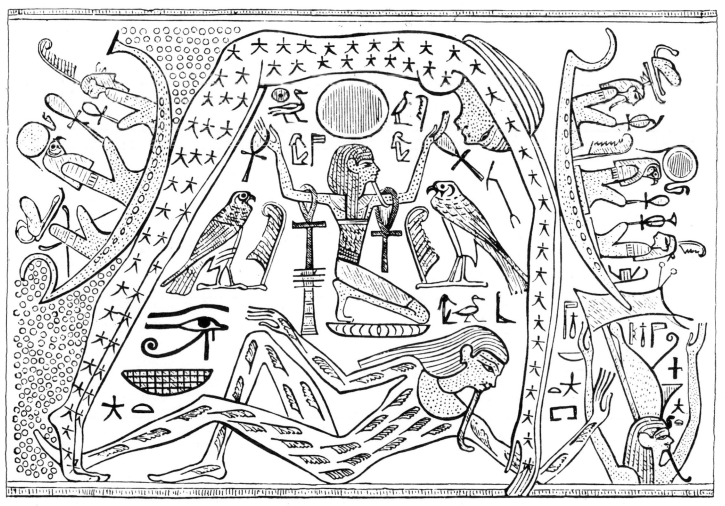

The cosmology. *Countries of the World*

Egyptian Designs continued

Monolith from the Temple of Philoe, with two border designs from the same temple. *L'Art, Vol. 16*

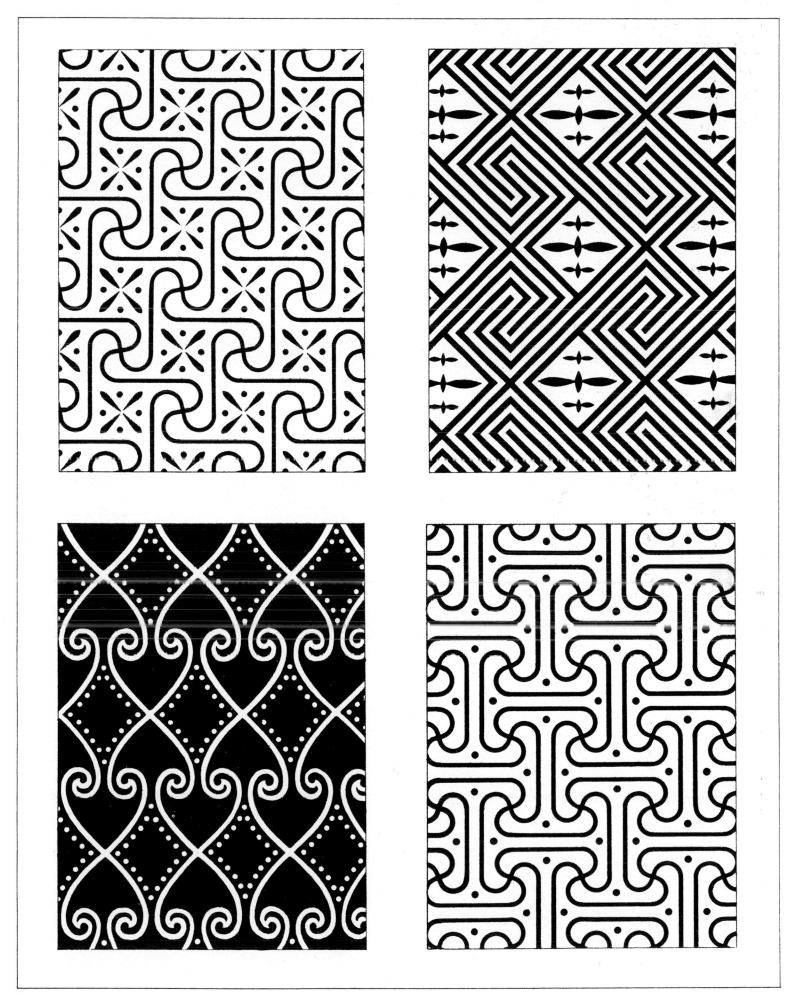

Diaper ornament. *Outlines*

Egyptian Designs continued

Painting of Anukeh and Ramses,
from an Egyptian temple. *Century, Vol. 13*

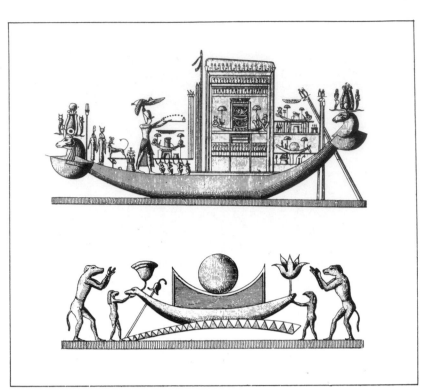

Sacred ships. *Source Illustrations*

Painting of a hawk. *Meyer's*

Ceremonial headdresses. *Costumes*

Egyptian jewelry. *Jewelry*

Egyptian Designs continued

Tomb painting. *Hart Publishing*

Mural tablet at Gebel Silsilis. *Century, Vol. 38*

Frieze from the Temple of Denderah Tentyris. *L'Art, Vol. 16*

Egyptian Designs continued

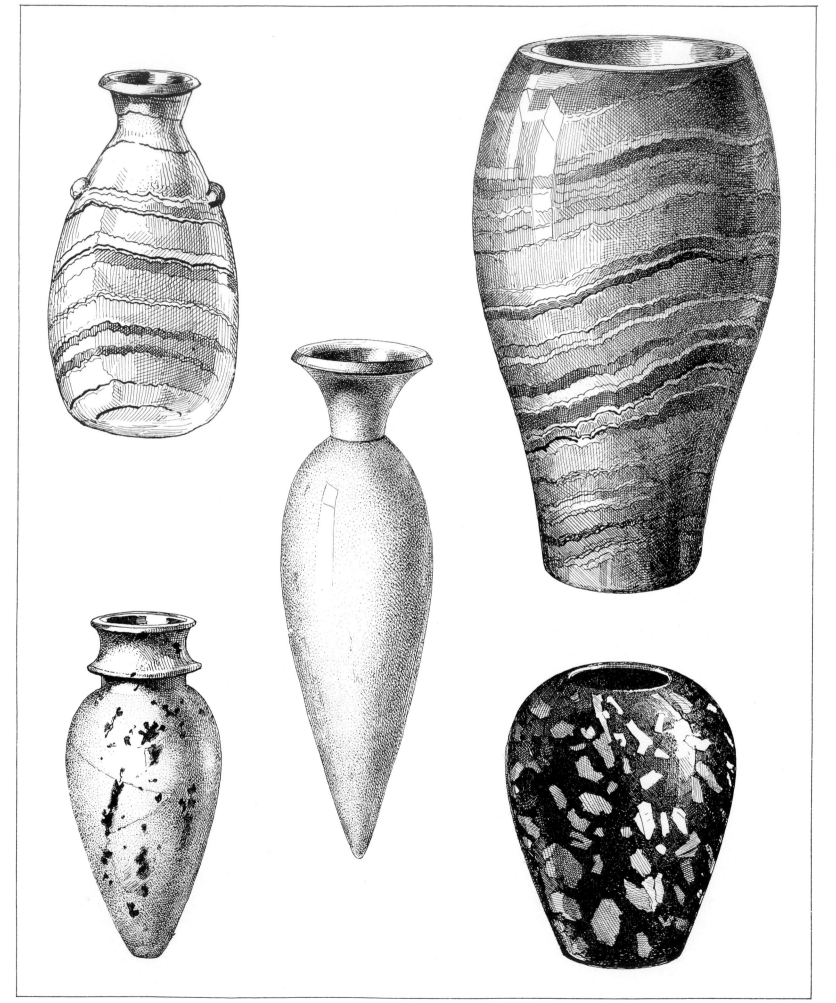

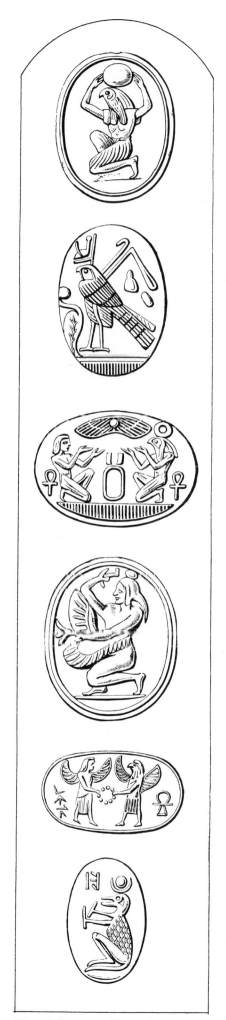

Apotheosis of Ramses II. The king is seated upon his throne while three gods (Amen-Ra-Tum, Safekh, and Tahut) are engaged in inscribing his name upon the fruits of the Tree of Life. *Century, Vol. 13*

Phoenician medallions. *Cyprus*

Apis, the sacred bull of Memphis. *Industrial Arts*

Egyptian Designs continued

Granite statue. *L'Art, Vol. 18*

Diaper ornament. *Outlines*

Various Egyptian designs. *Hart Publishing*

French Designs

Embroidery on crimson silk featuring St. Luke, 18th century, with details. *L'Art, Vol. 16*

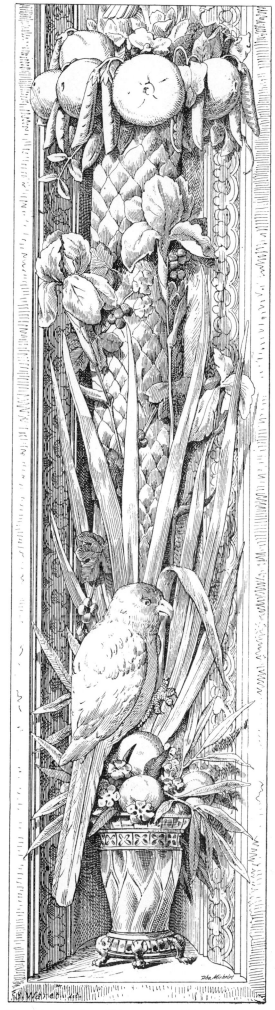

Hand-painted plate by the Cazin brothers, early 20th century. *L'Art, Vol. 37*

Tapestry border, 17th century. *L'Art, Vol. 20*

Composition by M. Emile Cause, 19th century. *L'Art, Vol. 31*

French Designs continued

Tragic masks, Paris Opera House. *Gewerbehalle, Vol. 9*

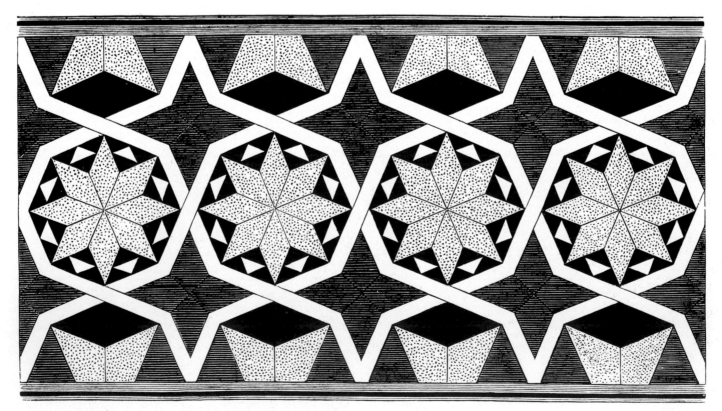

Mosaic in the cathedral of Monreale, 12th century. *Gewerbehalle, Vol. 10*

Paneling for a vestibule, 19th century. *Gewerbehalle, Vol. 10*

French Designs continued

Two geometrical designs. *L'Art, Vol. 14*

Vignettes from a pavement. *L'Art, Vol. 12*

Composition with mice, by M.D. Alliot of the National School of Design. *L'Art, Vol. 35*

Ceramic border. *L'Art, Vol. 27*

Conventional foliage. *Outlines*

French Designs continued

Textile pattern, 19th century. *L'Art Vol. 16*

Border design. *Outlines*

Tapestry ornament. *L'Art, Vol. 26*

Conventional foliage, from tapestries. *Outlines*

A pair of stained glass windows from the Church of *Saint Jean aux Bois*, near Compiegne, dating from the 13th century. *L'Art, Vol. 7*

French Designs continued

Various radial designs. *Gewerbehalle, Vol. 11*

A pair of floral motifs by Elisabeth Voysard. *L'Art, Vol. 5*

Gothic relief, Notre Dame Cathedral. *Gewerbehalle, Vol. 3*

French Designs continued

Conventional foliage. *Outlines*

Silver and enamel box shown at the Vienna World's Fair. *Gewerbehalle, Vol. 12*

Bookcover by Petit & Massard of Paris. *Workshop, Vol. 4*

French Designs continued

Book cover, 16th century. *L'Art, Vol. 8*

Book cover bearing the Montmorency coat of arms, 16th century. *L'Art, Vol. 5*

French Designs continued

A pair of "twines", or interlaced designs. *L'Art, Vol. 5*

Textile pattern, 19th century. *L'Art, Vol. 16*

Painted tissue, 18th century. *L'Art, Vol. 4*

French Designs continued

Enamel basin, 13th century. *L'Art, Vol. 18*

Flemish funeral slab, 15th century. *L'Art, Vol. 22*

French Designs continued

Facing ornamented manuscript pages, 17th century. *L'Art, Vol. 21*

French Designs continued

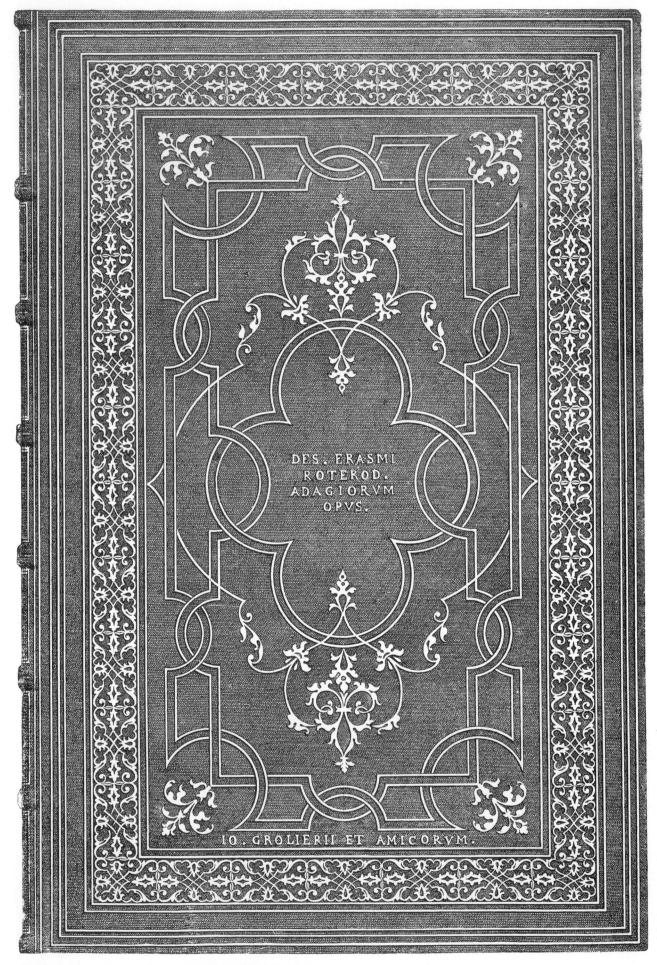

Book cover, tooled gold on green sheep-leather, 16th century. *L'Art, Vol. 22*

Coffer in tooled leather, with unicorn and stag, 15th century. *L'Art, Vol. 21*

French Designs continued

Flemish printed tissue, 14th century. *L'Art, Vol. 22*

Ornate Archbishop's crozier, 12th century, with detail. *L'Art, Vol. 24*

French Designs continued

Flemish wallpaper design, 18th century. *L'Art, Vol. 47*

Norman chimera, 14th century. *L'Art, Vol. 16*

Norman pilaster, 12th century. *Encyclopedia of Ornament*

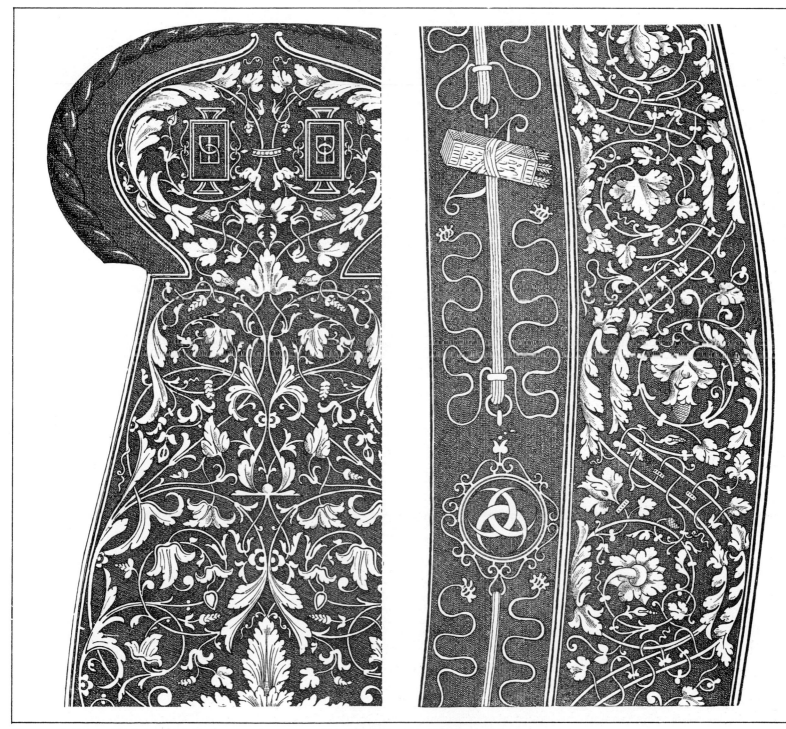

Ornamentation on the legs of a suit of armor, damascened in gold, 16th century. *L'Art, Vol. 9*

French Designs continued

Cartouche designed by A. Denvelle. *Workshop, Vol. 6*

Modern diaper. *Outlines*

French Designs continued

Medallian glass, 13th century, Saint Chapelle, Paris. *Glazier.*

Glazier.

Damask curtain. *Crystal Palace.*

Silver claret-jug decorated with enamel.
Crystal Palace.

Dark wood cabinet inlaid with marble and stone. *Crystal Palace.*

German Designs continued

Berlin tapestry in the Moresque style, early 19th century. *Gewerbehalle, Vol. 6*

Medieval fabric design. *Gewerbehalle, Vol. 2*

Austrian border design by Friedrich Fischbach. *Gewerbehalle, Vol. 3*

German Designs continued

Album cover exhibited at the Vienna World's Fair. *Gewerbehalle, Vol. 8*

A pair of designs by Professor Herdtle of Stuttgart. *Gewerbehalle, Vol. 2*

Diaper from a painting by Burkmaier, late 15th century. *Workshop, Vol. 2*

German Designs continued

Tapestry design. *Gewerbehalle, Vol. 5*

St. Stephen's dalmatic, 13th century, with detail. *L'Art, Vol. 24*

German Designs continued

Hand-painted plate. *Workshop, Vol. 8*

Embroidered valance, gold on red, 16th century. *Gewerbehalle, Vol. 8*

Gothic stonework.
Encyclopedia of Ornament

Vignette by Professor F. Fischbach of Hanau. *Workshop, Vol. 13*

Floor design, in marble, 16th century. *Gewerbehalle, Vol. 2*

German Designs continued

Painting dated 1472. *Encyclopedia of Ornament*

Border of a vase. *Gewerbehalle, Vol. 6*

Furniture ornament. *Gewerbehalle, Vol. 9*

German Designs continued

Medieval Dutch diaper. *Outlines*

Woven fabric, 15th century. *Gewerbehalle, Vol. 6*

Greek Designs

Terra cotta ornament. *Gewerbehalle, Various Vols.*

Terra cotta ornament. *Gewerbehalle, Various Vols.*

Greek Designs continued

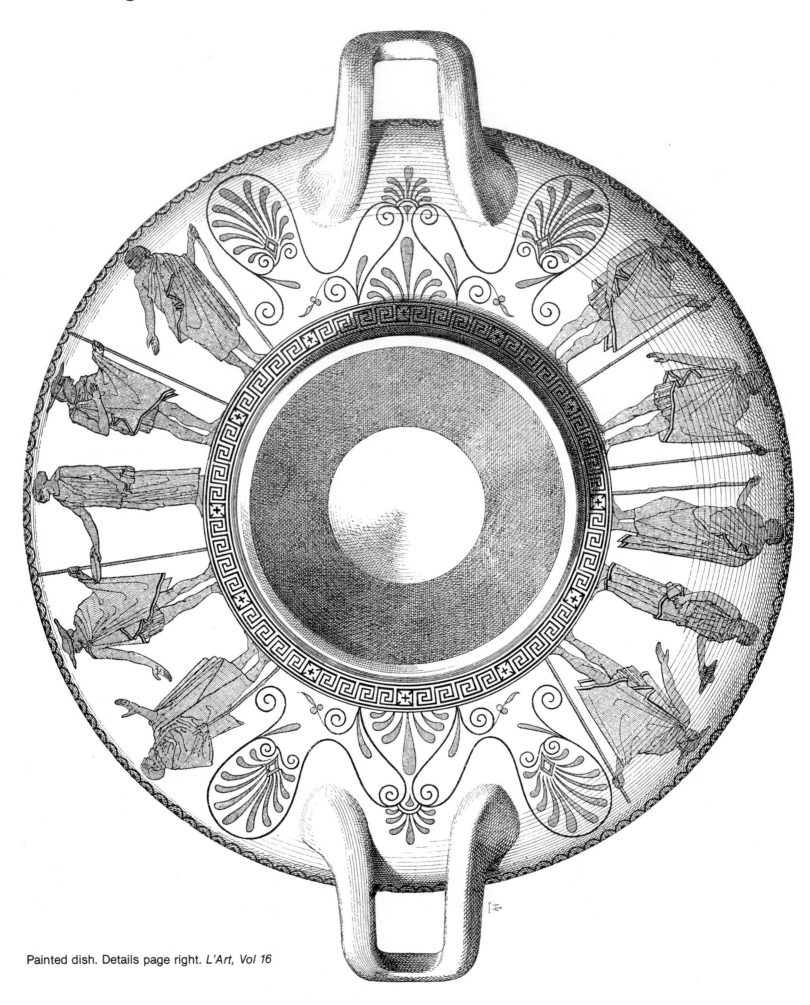

Painted dish. Details page right. *L'Art, Vol 16*

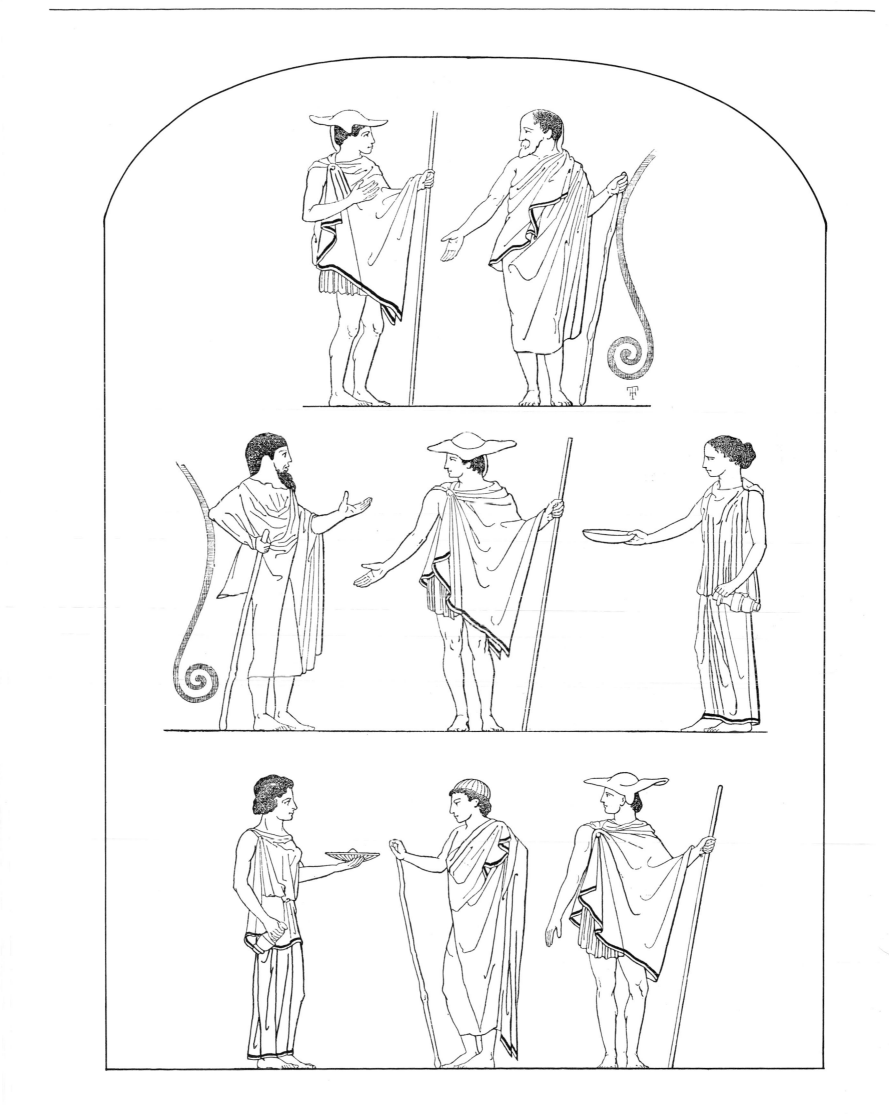

Greek Designs continued

Bas-relief depicting the Curetti striking their shields in order to drown the wailings of the infant Jupiter. *L'Art, Vol. 9*

Various fans. *L'Art, Vol. 39*

Anthropomorphic rhytons. *L'Art, Vol. 26 & 27*

Indian Designs continued

Manuscript ornament. *L'Art*

Sixteenth century tapestry. *L'Art, Vol. 32*

Cotton print pattern. *Pattern Design*

Cotton print pattern. *Pattern Design*

Indian Designs continued

Cotton print pattern. *Pattern Design*

Cotton print pattern. *Pattern Design*

E. Wallet. sc.

Painted tissue, 17th century. *L'Art, Vol. 22*

Indian Designs continued

18th century, India. *Glazier.*

Glazier.

India, circa 1750. *Bizarre Designs.*

Italian Designs

Floor mosaic, Palermo Cathedral. *Gewerbehalle, Vol. 6*

Wainscoting in the sacristy of Santa Maria Cathedral, Verona. *Workshop, Vol. 2*

Linen design, 19th century. *Gewerbehalle, Vol. 3*

Italian Designs continued

Italian Designs continued

Fabric design. *Gewerbehalle, Vol. 10*

Frame designed by Rinaldo Barbetti, 19th century. *Workshop, Vol. 6*

Italian Designs continued

Dish, 16th century, shown actual size. *L'Art, Vol. 24*

Late Gothic design, taken from a painting by Ambrogio Fossano, dated 1490. *Gewerbehalle, Vol. 2*

Ceramic border design. *Workshop, Vol. 7*

Italian Designs continued

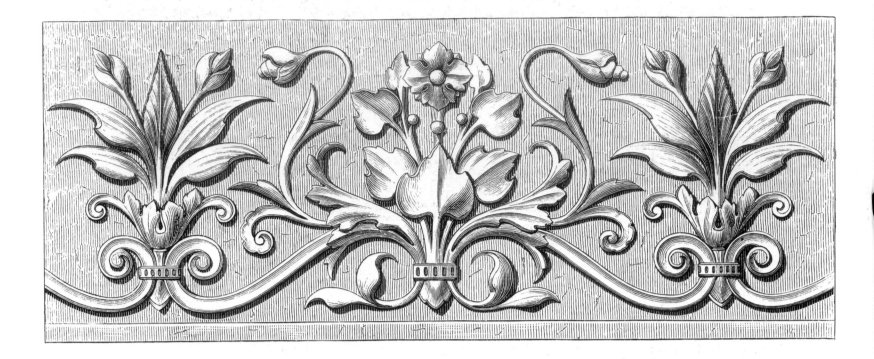

Renaissance ornament, two examples. *Gewerbehalle, Vol. 5*

Gothic fabric showing Saracenic influence, late 12th century. *Period Furnishings*

Italian Designs continued

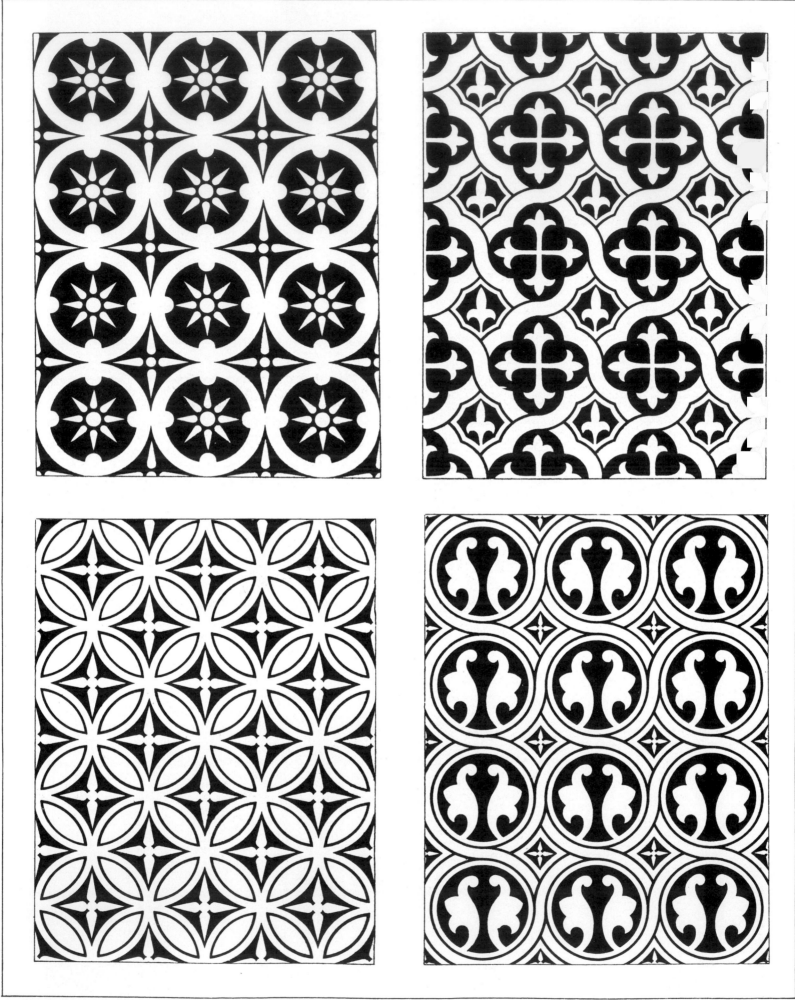

Medieval Sicilian diaper. *Outlines*

Hand-painted Sicilian dish, 15th century. *L'Art, Vol. 16*

Italian Designs continued

Sicilian fabric, 13th century. *Glazier.*

Naples, 1436. *Symbols, Signs & Signets.*

Sicilian fabric, 13th century. *Glazier.*

Sicilian fabric, 13th century. *Glazier.*

Fabric design, Italy. *Glazier.*

Sicilian fabric, 13th century. *Glazier.*

16th century fabric, Italy. *Glazier.*

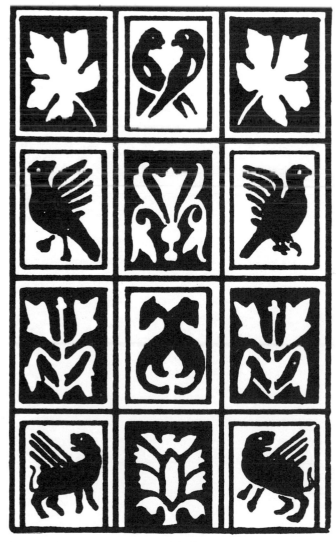

Sicilian fabric, 13th century. *Glazier.*

Sicilian fabric, 13th century. *Glazier.*

Japanese Designs continued

Tissues with star motifs. *L'Art, Vol. 28*

Bird folk motif, in bronze. *L'Art, Vol. 14*

Ancient tapestry design. *L'Art, Vol. 37*

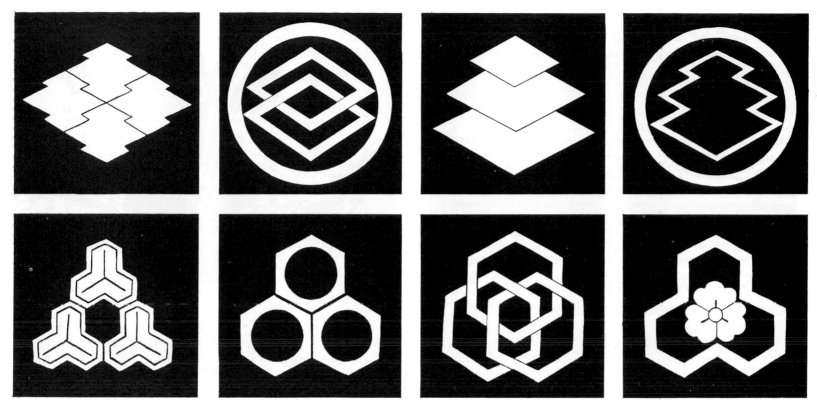

Motifs from family crests. *Design Motifs*

Japanese Stencil Designs

Japanese Designs continued

Variations on two motifs taken from ancient family crests; *top*, flower diamond motifs; *bottom*, gingko leaf motifs.   *Design Motifs*

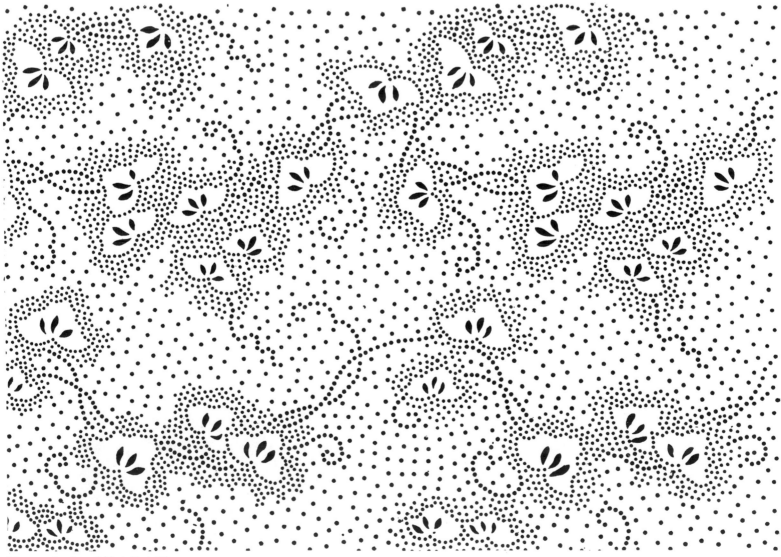

Tissue design. *L'Art. Vol. 28*

Powdered ornament. *Outlines*

Two hand-painted plates, early 20th century. *L'Art, Vol. 31*

Water color by celebrated artist Hokou Sai. *L'Art, Vol. 27*

Japanese Designs continued

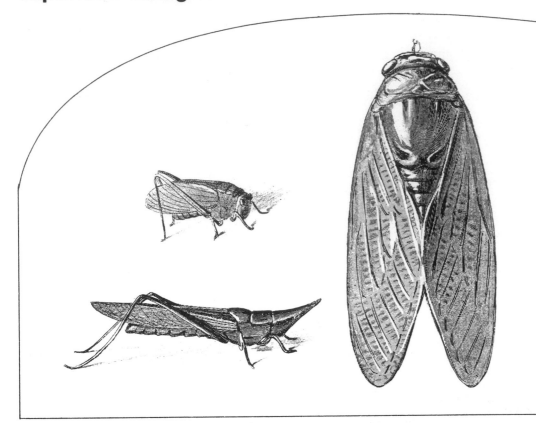

Insect folk motifs, in bronze. *L'Art, Vol. 31*

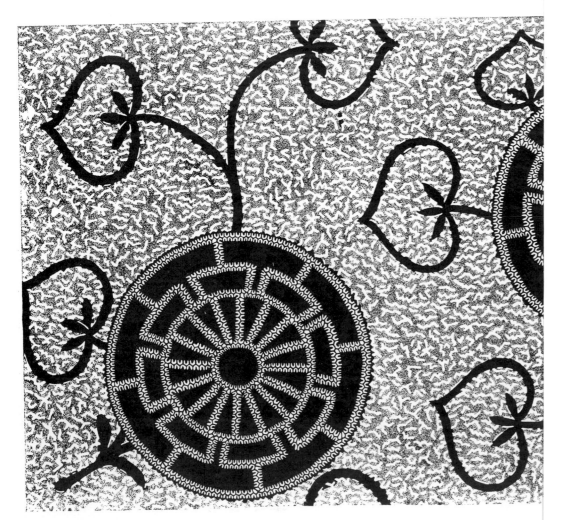

Tissue design. *L'Art, Vol. 29*

Japanese Designs continued

Ink drawing. *Hachi-jo*

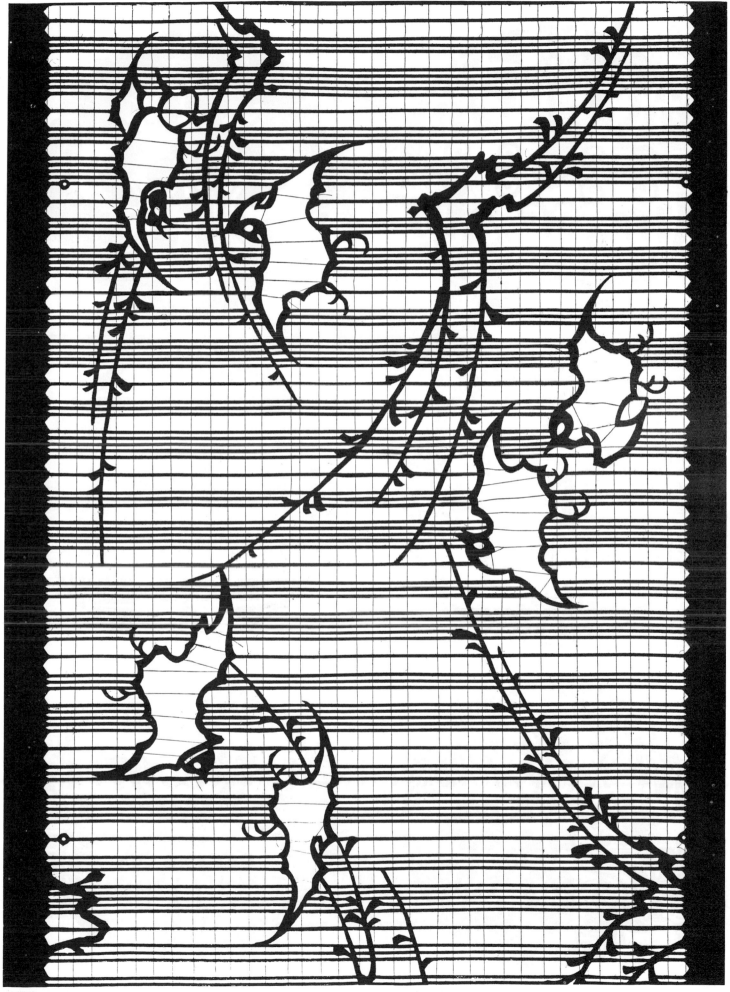

Tissue design. *L'Art, Vol. 26*

Japanese Designs continued

Japanese stencil of umbrellas with characters and crests of owners.
Japanese Stencil Designs

Glazier.

Glazier.

Japanese crests from 1900 on. *Symbols, Signs & Signets.*

Japanese Designs continued

Japanese Stencil Designs

Japanese Stencil Designs

Tissue design. *L'Art, Vol. 29* ☐

Seventeenth century sword guards. *L'Art*

Mexican Designs

Stamp of "flint serpent" design. *Design Motifs*

Variation on "blue worm" design. *Design Motifs*

Cylindrical stamp. *Design Motifs*

Aztec Design. *Source unknown*

Flat stamp from Mexico City. *Design Motifs*

From a Mayan Manuscript.
Source unknown

Mexican Designs continued

Aztec design. *Source unknown*

Flat stamp from Azapotzalco.
Design Motifs

Painting of parchment, Mixtec, Mexico. *Source unknown*

Mexican Designs continued

Mayan war-god. *Century*

Mayan rain-god. *Century*

Modern Mexican tiles showing Aztec influence. *Source unknown*

"Covatl" or "serpent monster," Vera Cruz, Mexico. *Source unknown*

Cylindrical stamp from Mexico City. *Design Motifs*

Mexican Designs continued

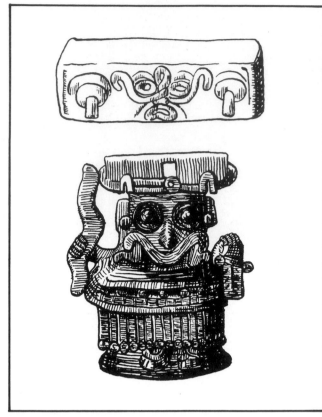

Mayan representations of *Tlalok* on pottery. *Origins*

Design showing dedication of the temple of *Huitzilipochtli,* the Aztec god of war. *Source unknown*

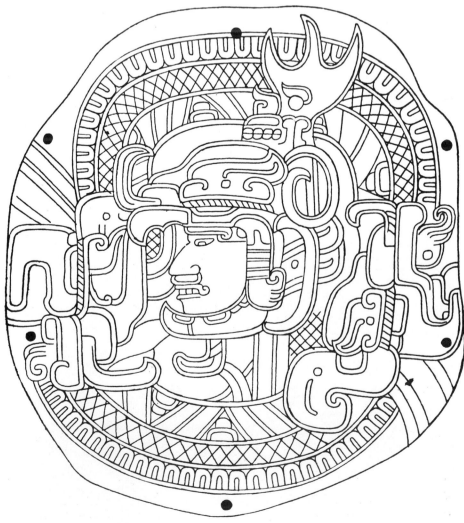

Mexican design carved on a turtle shell. *Source unknown*

Mayan vases found at Cuecuetenanco. *Incidents*

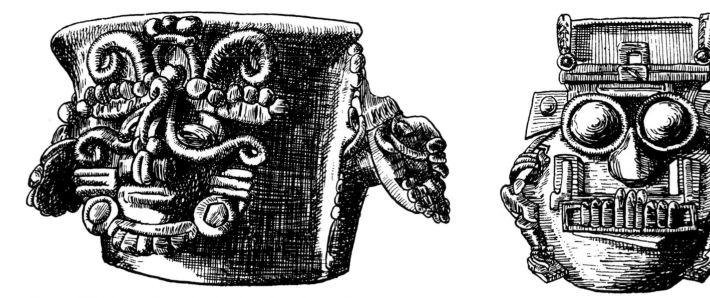

Figure of *Tlalok* on a piece of pottery from Quen Santo. *Origins*

Figure of *Tlalok* from Tlaxcala. *Origins*

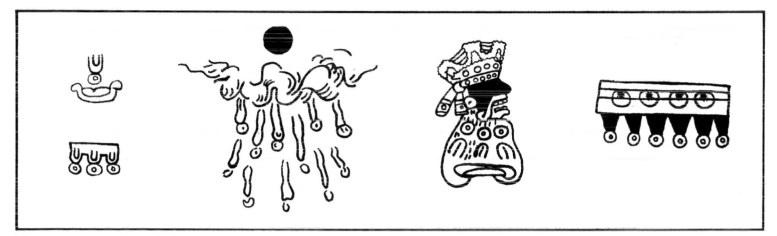

Mayan representations of rain. *Origins*

Decoration from an ancient Mayan vase. *Origins*

Panamanian Designs

Vase with peccary form. *Ethnology*

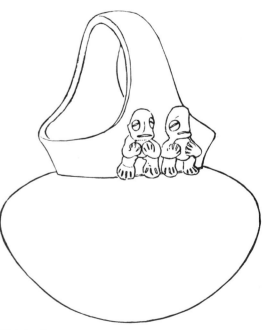

Chiriquian statuette. *Ethnology*

Odd shaped vase. *Ethnology*

Chiriquian vase with arched handles.
Ethnology

Chiriquian battle with arched panels. *Ethnology*

Underside of a vase. *Ethnology*

Chiriquian statuettes of the alligator group. *Ethnology*

Pennsylvania Dutch Designs

Sgraffito plate design. *Source unknown*

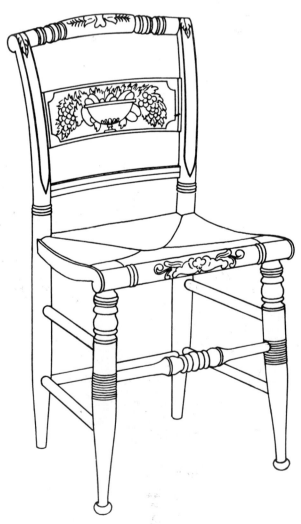

Chair with Pennsylvania Dutch inspired designs.
Source unknown

Various bird motifs. *Source unknown*

Decoration from a Pennsylvania Dutch chest. *Source unknown*

Turned wood spice boxes.
Source unknown

Marks of Pennsylvania Dutch craftsmen. *Source unknown*

Pennsylvania Designs continued

Pennsylvania Dutch hex signs and embroidery designs. *Symbols*

Design from a Pennsylvania
Dutch plate. *Early American*

Pennsylvania Dutch design. *Early American*

Barn with hex signs, Lehigh County, Pennsylvania. *Source unknown*

Pennsylvania Dutch balloon-back chair. *Source unknown*

Pennsylvania Dutch spoon rack. *Source unknown*

Pennsylvania Designs continued

Design with birds and flowers. *Folk Art Motifs*

Various bird designs. *Folk Art Motifs*

Persian Designs continued

Ancient jade screen with gems set in gold. *L'Art, Vol. 9*

Drawing by Mirza Akbar, early 10th century. *Pattern Design*

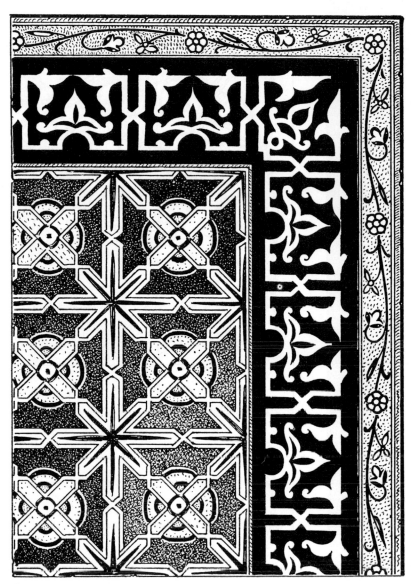

Carpet design, 14th century. *Pattern Design*

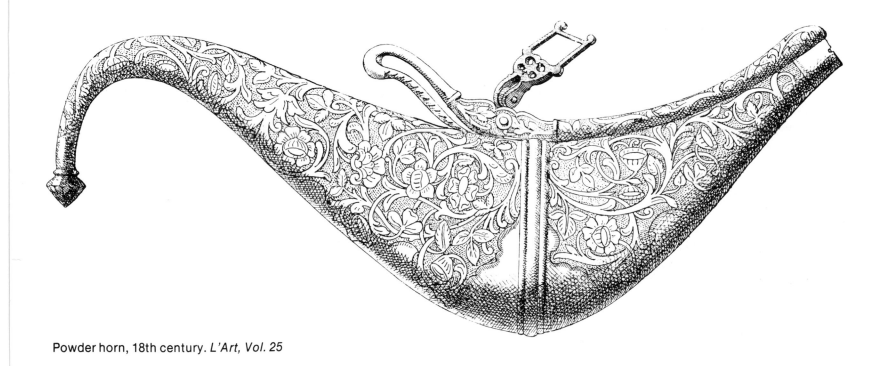

Powder horn, 18th century. *L'Art, Vol. 25*

Persian Designs continued

Carpet Design, 14th century. *Pattern Design*

Islamic silk design, 14th century. *Pattern Design*

Woven silk fabric, 17th century. *Pattern Design*

Conventional foliage. *Pattern Design*

Persian Designs continued

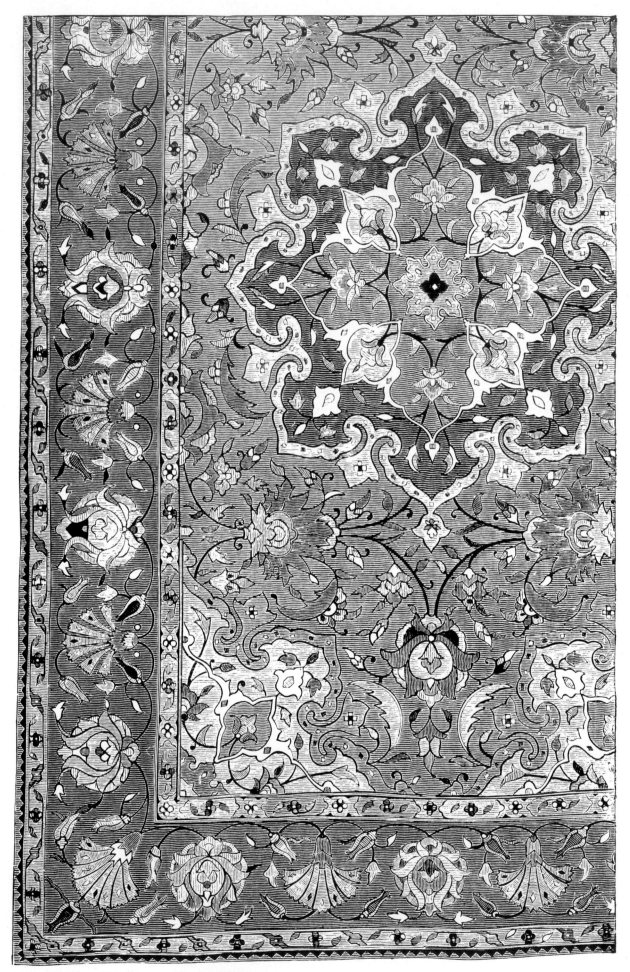

Carpet design, 16th century. *Industrial Arts*

Ceramic ornament, 18th century. *L'Art, Vol. 27*

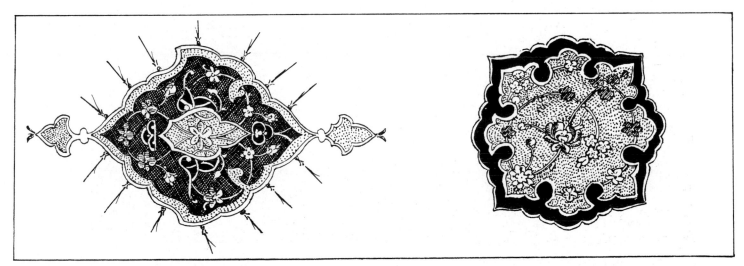

Arabic manuscript ornament. *L'Art, Vol. 18*

Persian Designs continued

Drawing by Mirza Akbar, early 19th century. *Pattern Design*

Palmette pattern on enameled bricks, 6th century b.c. *Pattern Design*

Ceramic ornament, 18th century. *L'Art, Vol. 27*

Star-shaped pavements. *L'Art, Vol. 24*

Persian Designs continued

Axe heads ornamented with gold, 18th century. *Weapons and Armor*

Assyrian pavement, 17th century. L'Art, Vol. 25

Wall tile designs, 16th century. *Pattern Design*

Detail of a 16th century carpet, in silk. *Hart Publishing*

Motifs from a Persian carpet found in perpetual ice in the Soviet Union, over 2400 years old. *Hart Publishing*

Persian Designs continued

Designs on various gun barrels, 19th century. *L'Art, Vol. 47*

Hand-painted plates, 16th century. *L'Art, Vol. 41*

Persian Designs continued

Arabic manuscript page. *Hart Publishing*

L'Art, Vol. 16

Arabesques. *L'Art, Vol. 27*

Ornamental shield. *L'Art, Vol. 12*

Miniature painting. *Harper's*

Arabesques. *L'Art, Vol. 17*

Manuscript ornaments.
L'Art, Vol. 8

Embroidered cloth. *Harper's*

Persian Designs continued

A Treasury of Design.

Wall tiles. *Glazier.*

Glazier.

Earthenware from Rhodes, 15th century. *Glazier*

Glazier.

Glazier.

Persian Designs continued

16th century Persian carpet. *Glazier.*

A Treasury of Design.

Peruvian Designs

Assorted Chimu vases. *I.L.E.*

Assorted Chimu vases. *I.L.E.*

Peruvian Designs continued

Peruvian ceramics. *American Continent*

Ornamental block of stone from a Peruvian temple. *Source unknown*

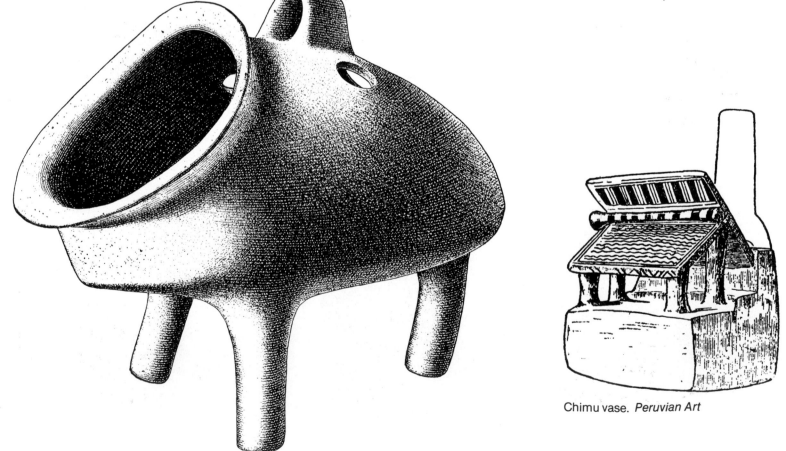

Three-legged brazier from Machu Picchu. *Source unknown*

Chimu vase. *Peruvian Art*

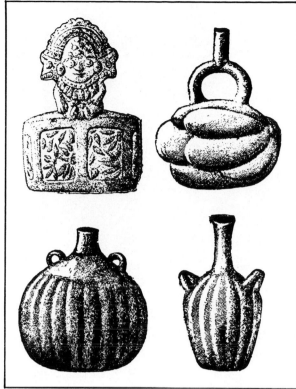

Peruvian ceramics. *American Continent*

Two-handled dish used by Incas to serve food. *Source unknown*

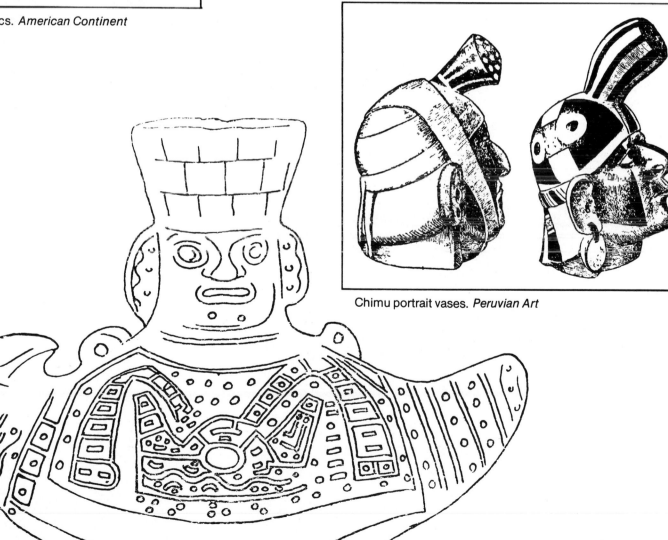

Chimu portrait vases. *Peruvian Art*

Typical vase from Recuay. *Source unknown*

Peruvian Designs continued

Dragon design from a painted pitcher, Truxillo. *Source unknown*

Peruvian design. *Source unknown*

Design from bowls of Nazca, Peru. *Source unknown*

Peruvian design. *Source unknown*

Peruvian design. *Source unknown*

Peruvian Designs continued

Glazier.

Glazier.

Glazier.

Glazier.

Glazier.

Glazier.

Glazier.

Glazier.

Glazier.

Glazier.

Pompeian Designs

Frieze from Pompeii. *Glazier.*

Pavement, 2nd century Vatican. *Glazier.*

Painted pilaster from Pompeii. *Glazier.*

Ancient Roman mosaic floor. *Glazier.*

Mosaic floor. *Glazier.*

Wall decoration, Forum of Hercules,
Pompeii, 79 A.D. *Glazier.*

Mosaic floor. *Glazier.*

Roman Designs

Sarcophagus of Alexander Severus and Mamaea. *Roman People*

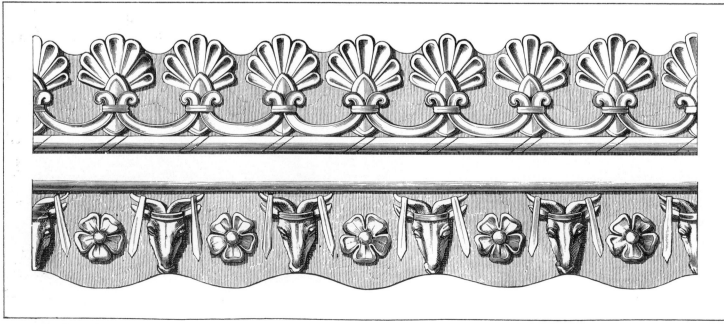

Border designs in terra cotta. *Workshop, Vol. 3*

Design on a drinking vessel. *Gewerbehalle, Vol. 5*

Roman Designs continued

Marble flower from the Forum of Nerva. *Gewerbehalle, Vol. 11*

Imperial Roman eagle, in marble. *Gewerbehalle, Vol. 4*

Cornice ornament in marble from the Temple of Jupiter Tonans. *Workshop, Vol. 10*

Roman Designs continued

Silver vase. *L'Art, Vol. 21*

Marble statue of Augustus. *L'Art, Vol. 12*

Roman Designs continued

Vase in the shape of a rhyton. *L'Art, Vol. 22*

Rosettes. *Workshop, Vol. 8*

Terra cotta antefixes. *Gewerbehalle, Vol. 9*

Terra cotta frieze. *Workshop, Vol. 4*

Roman Designs continued

Dress of Roman generals. *Costumes*

Kraters engraved with ivy. *Workshop, Vol. 6*

Bronze mask of Bacchus, shown actual size. *L'Art, Vol. 22*

Roman Designs continued

Fragment from a frieze depicting Leda and the swan. *L'Art. Vol. 12*

Scandinavian Designs

Norwegian ornaments. *New York Public Library.*

Norwegian wood carving.

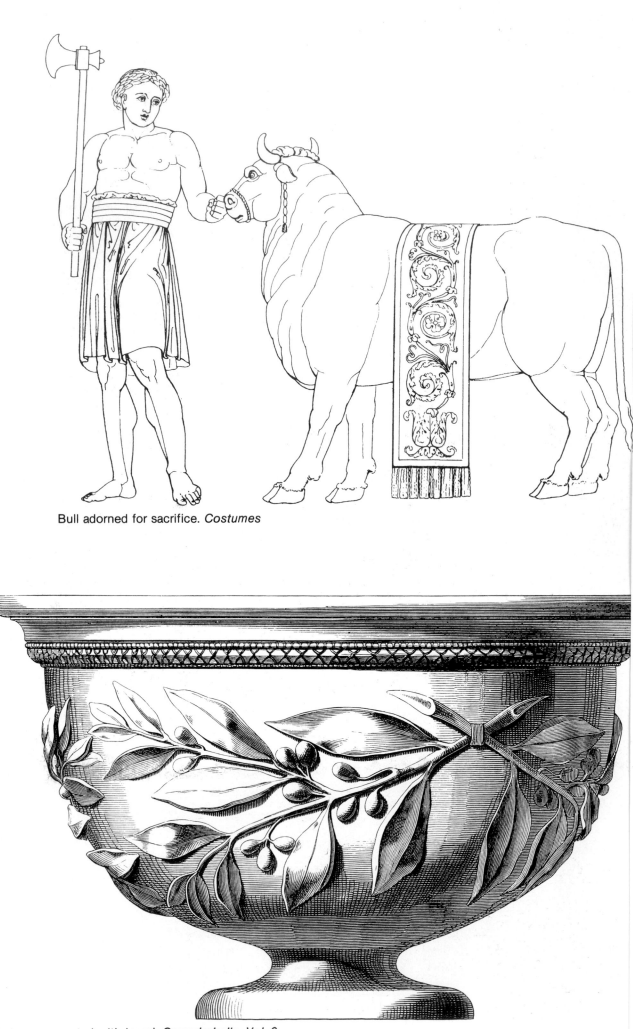

Bull adorned for sacrifice. *Costumes*

Krater ornamented with laurel. *Gewerbehalle, Vol. 9*

Carved lid of Norwegian bridal chest. *New York Public Library.*

Norwegian wood carving.

Norwegian ornament.

Scandinavian Designs continued

Swedish designs. *New York Public Library*.

Swiss pattern designs. *Das Ornament Werk*

Slavic Designs

Krausauskas.

The Art of the Book

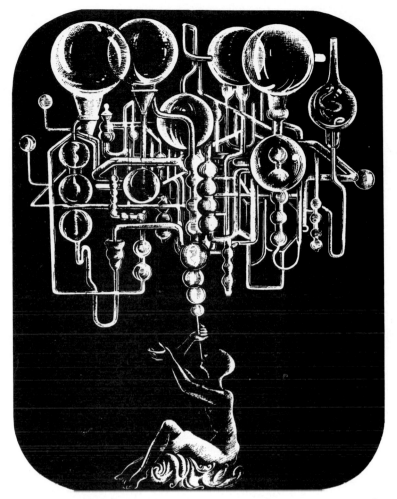

Art of the Book.

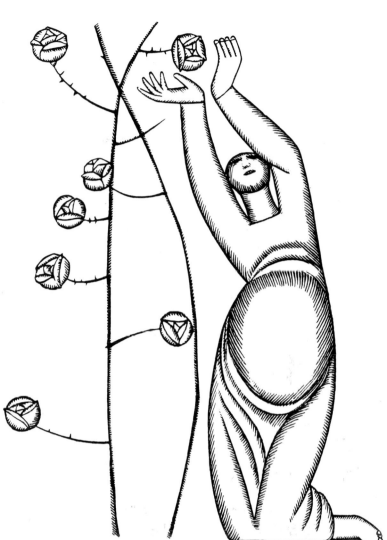

Art of the Book.

Krausauskas.

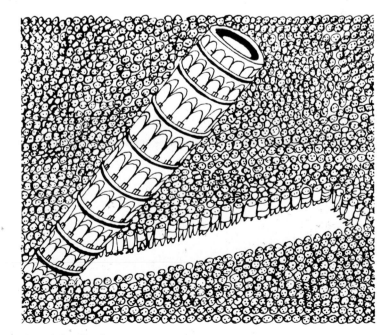

Art of the Book.

Slavic Designs continued

Grafika.

Art of the Book.

Slavic Designs continued

Pikov.

Pikov.

Krausauskas.

Pikov.

Art of the Book.

Art of the Book.

Art of the Book

Art of the Book.

Art of the Book.

Slavic Designs continued

Pikov.

Pikov.

Pikov.

Pikov.

Pikov.

Art of the Book.

Art of the Book.

Art of the Book.

Art of the Book.

SOURCES

AFRICAN DESIGNS. Williams, Geoffrey. New York: Dover Publications, 1971.

ALLOVER PATTERNS; full title, *Allover Patterns for Designers and Craftsmen.* New York: Dover Publications, Inc., 1975.

AMERICAN CONTINENT; full title, *The American Continent and Its Inhabitants Before Its Discovery by Columbus.* Cady, Annie Cole. Philadelphia: Gebbie, 1890.

APPLIED ARTS. From a portfolio of craft designs. No date.

ARABIA. A pottery manufacturing firm in Finland.

ART OF THE BOOK 1961-1962, THE. Moscow: 1967

ART JOURNAL. New York: James S. Virtue, 1854-1861.

ARTISTIC JAPAN; full title, *Artistic Japan, a Monthly Illustrated Journal of the Arts and Industries.* S. Low. London: 1888-1891.

AUTHENTIC INDIAN DESIGNS. Naylor, Maria, ed. New York: Dover Publications, 1975.

BAMBOO STUDIO (four vols.). Fun Cheng Yeu. Peking: World Book Company, 1952.

BIZARRE DESIGNS; full title, *Bizarre Designs in Silks.* Slomann, Vilhelm. Copenhagen, Denmark: Munksgaard, no date.

BOURGOIN; full title, *Arabic Geometrical Pattern and Design.* Bourgoin, J. New York: Dover Publications, 1973.

BRITISH MUSEUM. England.

BUDAPEST MUSEUM. Budapest, Hungary.

CENTURY; full title, *The Century Illustrated Monthly Magazine.* New York: The Century Company, 1883-1913.

CHICAGO NATURAL HISTORY MUSEUM. Chicago, Illinois

CHINESE FOLK DESIGNS. Hawley, W.M. New York: Dover Publications, 1949.

CHINESISCHE TEPPICH, DER. Hackmack, Adolf. Hamburg: Fredrichsen, c. 1920.

COPTIC TEXTILE DESIGNS. Gerspach, M. New York: Dover Publications, 1975.

COSTUMES; full title, *Costumes of the Greeks and Romans.* Hope, Thomas. New York: Dover Publications, 1962.

COUNTRIES OF THE WORLD (six vols.). Brown, Robert. London: Cassell and Company, Ltd., no date.

CRYSTAL PALACE; full title, *Crystal Palace Exhibition.* New York: Dover Publications, 1970.

CYPRUS; full title, *Cyprus; Its Ancient Cities, Tombs, and Temples.* Cesnola, Luigi Palma di. New York: Harper, 1878.

DAS ORNAMENT WERK. Bossert, Verlag Ernst Wasmuth. Berlin: circa 1902.

DECORATIVE ART; full title, *Decorative Art of the Southwestern Indians.* Sides, Dorothy Smith. New York: Dover Publications, 1961.

DESIGN AND DECORATION; full title, *American Indian Design and Decoration.* Appleton, Leroy H. New York: Dover Publications, 1971.

DESIGN FOR SCHOOLS; full title, *Design for Schools: A Handbook for Teachers.* Holland, Charles. London: Macmillan & Co., Ltd., 1907.

DESIGN MOTIFS. Mizoguchi, Saburo. Tokyo: Shibundo, 1973.

DESIGN MOTIFS; full title, *Design Motifs of Ancient Mexico.* Enciso, Jorge. New York: Dover Publications, 1953.

EARLY AMERICAN; full title, *Early American Design Motifs.* Chapman, Suzanne E. New York: Dover Publications, 1974.

EHMCKE; full title, *Graphic Trade Symbols by German Designers.* Ehmcke, F.H. ed. New York: Dover Publications, 1974.

ENCYCLOPEDIA OF ORNAMENT, THE. Shaw, Henry. Edinburgh: 1842

ENCYCLOPEDIA OF SOURCE ILLUSTRATIONS. Heck, J.G., ed. London: Morgan & Morgan, 1972.

ENCYCLOPEDIE; full title, *Encyclopedie*

des Metiers d'Art. Paris: Albert Morance, no date.

ENGLISH ENCYCLOPEDIA: *A Collection of Treatises Illustrative of the Arts and Sciences* (10 vols.). London: G. Kearsley of Fleet Street, 1802.

ESTONIAN GRAPHICS. Mal'kova, Yu., ed. Moscow:Sov. Khudozhnik, 1972

ETHNOLOGY; full title, *Bureau of Ethnology Annual Reports.* Washington, D.C.: Smithsonian Institution, c. 1895.

FOLK ART MOTIFS; full title, *Folk Art Motifs of Pennsylvania.* Lichten, Frances, New York: Dover Publications, 1954.

FOLK DESIGNS; full title, *Chinese Folk Designs.* Hawley, W.M. New York: Dover Publications, 1971.

GEWERBEHALLE: *Organ fur den Fortschritt in allen Zweigen der Kunst-Industrie.* Schnorr, Julius, ed. Vienna: 1862-1883.

GLASS; full title, *Early American Pressed Glass Patterns.* Lee, Ruth Webb. Northboro, Mass.: Ruth Webb Lee, c. 1931.

GLAZIER; full title, *A Manual of Historic Ornament.* Glazier, R., ed. London: B.T. Batsford, 1899.

GRAFIKA; full title, *Zsmonskaya Grafika.* Isdatyeelbstvo "Sovyetskie Khoodaozhnik." Moscow: 1964.

HACHI-JO; full title, *History of the Isle of Hachi-jo.* Hobusai. Tokyo, 1816.

HARPER'S; full title, *Harper's New Monthly Magazine.* New York: Harper & Brothers, 1851-1888.

HISTORIC ORNAMENT (two vols.). Ward, James. London: Chapman & Hall, 1897.

I.L.E.; full title, *Illustracion Espanola y Americana.* Madrid: c. 1860.

INCIDENTS; full title, *Incidents of Travel in Central America, Chiapas, and Yucatan.* New York: Harpers, 1841.

INDUSTRIAL ARTS; full title, *Chefs-D'Oeuvre of the Industrial Arts.* Burty, Phillipe. New York: D. Appleton & Company, 1869.

INDUSTRY OF NATIONS; full title, *The Industry of All Nations,* (a special issue of the *Art Journal* devoted to the Crystal Palace Exhibition). London: George Virtue, 1851.

IOUIYA & TOUIYOU; full title, *The Tomb of Iouiya and Touiyou.* Davis, Theo. M. London: A. Constable, 1907.

JAPANESE STENCIL DESIGNS. Tuer, Andrew W. New York: Dover Publications, 1967.

JEWELRY. Sietsema, Robert. New York: Hart Publishing Company, 1978.

KRAUSAUSKAS; full title, *Stasys Krausauskas.* Vilna, 1972.

L'ART; full title, *L'Art Pour Tous, Encyclopedie de l'Art Industriel et Decoratif.* Reiber, Emile, ed. Paris: A. Morel et C., 1861-1906.

LA TOILE. Paris: c. 1900.

LA VIE PRIVEE; full title, *La vie privee des anciens* (four vols.). Paris: Morel, 1880-1900.

LIPTOV MUSEUM. Ruzomberok, Czechoslovakia.

LITHUANIAN GRAPHICS; full title, *Lithuanian Graphics, 1966-1967.* Vilnius, 1968.

LONDON NEWS; full title, *Illustrated London News.* London: George C. Leighton, 1866-1883.

LOTHROP; full title, *Pottery of Costa Rica and Nicaragua.* Lothrop, S.K. New York: Museum of the American Indian, 1926.

MENTEN; full title, *Art Nouveau & Early Art Deco Type & Design.* Menten, Theodore, ed. New York: Dover Publications, 1972.

METIERS D'ART; full title, *Histoire des meiers d'art.* Fontanes, Jean de. Paris: no date.

MEYERS; full title, *Meyers konnerlations-Lexikon.* Leipsig und Wein: Bibliographisches Institut, 1895.

MIMBRES DESIGNS; full title, *Mimbres Design Calendar.* Maxwell Museum of Anthropology, University of New Mexico, Albuquerque, New Mexico.

MUSEUM OF PRIMITIVE ART. New York.

NATURAL HISTORY; full title, *American Museum Journal.* New York: The American Museum of Natural History, c. 1900.

NEEDLE AND BRUSH; full title, *Needle and Brush: Useful and Decorative.* New York: Butterick Publishing Co., Ltd., 1899.

NEW YORK PUBLIC LIBRARY. New York.

ORIGINS; full title, *Mayan and Mexican Origins.* Cambridge, Mass.: privately printed, 1926.

OUTLINES; full title, *Outlines of Ornament in the Leading Styles.* Audsley, W. & G. New York: Scribner, 1882.

PAPERCUT DESIGN. Available from China Books and Periodicals. 125 Fifth Avenue, New York City.

PATTERN AND DESIGN; full title, *Pattern and Design with Dynamic Symmetry.* Edwards, Edward B. New York: Dover Publications, 1967.

PATTERN DESIGN; original title, *Traditional Methods of Pattern Designing.* Christie, Archibald H. New York: Dover Publications, 1967 (original publication date, 1910).

PERIOD FURNISHINGS: *An Encyclopedia of Ornament.* Clifford, C.R. New York: Clifford & Lawton, 1914.

PERUVIAN ART; full title, *Peruvian Art in the School.* Izcue, Elena. Paris: Editorial Excelsior, 1926.

PIKOV; full title, *Mikhail Ivanovich Pikov.* Moscow: Kuznetsova, 1971.

POLISH GRAPHIC ARTS; full title, *Essays on Polish Graphic Arts of the First Half of the 20th Century.* Tananaeva, Larisa Ivanovna. Moscow, 1972.

ROMAN PEOPLE; full title, *History of Rome and of the Roman People From Its Origin to the Invasion of the Barbarians.* Boston: Estes & Lauriat, 1890.

ROYAL ONTARIO MUSEUM OF ARCHAEOLOGY. Toronto, Canada.

SHORT HISTORY; full title, *A Short History of Art.* De Forest, A. & Julia B. New York: Phillips & Hunt, 1881.

SMITHSONIAN INSTITUTION. Washington, D.C.

STUDIO: *An Illustrated Magazine of Fine and Applied Art.* Longon: 1880-1902.

SUNDAY BOOK; full title, *The Pictorial Sunday Book.* Kitto, John, ed. London: The London Printing and Publishing Company, Ltd., no date.

SYMBOLS; full title, *American Symbols.* Lehner, Ernst, compiler. New York: William Penn Publishing Corp., 1966.

SYMBOLS, SIGNS & SIGNETS. Lehner, Ernst. New York: Dover Publications, 1969.

TREASURY OF DESIGN, A; full title, *A Treasury of Design for Artists and Craftsmen.* Mirow, Gregory. New York: Dover Publications, 1969.

TYPE & DESIGN; full title, *Art Nouveau & Early Art Deco Type & Design.* Menten, Theodore. New York: Dover Publications, 1972.

UNIVERSITY OF DUBLIN. Ireland

VICTORIAN STENCILS; full title, *Victorian Stencils for Design and Decoration.* Gillon, Edmund V. New York: Dover Publications, 1968.

VOYAGES AND TRAVELS (2 vols.). Calange. The Walker Company, no date.

WALLPAPER; full title, *Wards Wallpaper Catalog.* Baltimore, Md.: Montgomery Ward, c. 1950.

WEAPONS & ARMOR. Sietsema, Robert. New York: Hart Publishing Company, 1978.

WORKSHOP, THE: *A Monthly Journal, Devoted to Progress of the Useful Arts,* (English language edition of *Gewerbehalle*). Baumer, W., and J. Schnorr, eds. New York: E. Steiger, 1868-1883.